THE HERALD
DIARY

Owling with Laughter

THE HERALD DIARY

Owling with Laughter

Ken Smith

BLACK & WHITE PUBLISHING

First published 2020
by Black & White Publishing Ltd
Nautical House, 104 Commercial Street
Edinburgh, EH6 6NF

1 3 5 7 9 10 8 6 4 2   20 21 22 23

ISBN: 978 1 78530 317 3

A CIP catalogue record for this book is available from the British Library.

Typeset by Iolaire Typography, Newtonmore
Printed and bound by CPI Group (UK) Ltd, Croydon, CR0 4YY

Contents

Introduction

If ever there was a year when Scots had to show they had a keen sense of humour then it was this one. When even turning on the television news took fortitude and stoicism, everyone craved a moment of lightness to cheer up their days.

Fortunately, we have the good readers of *The Herald* newspaper, who have ensured the witticisms, daftness and belly-laughs they have heard or witnessed were always passed on to the newspaper's daily Diary column.

And we really need a laugh after what has befallen us, so to make it that extra bit special we have gone back ten years to bring together the very best of the Diary column from over the past decade.

These are the stories of Scots – stories they've heard or witnessed at work, in the street, on the train or in their own homes. They are well worth sharing and offer something to be enjoyed at any time.

1

I Belong to Glasgow

There has always been a lively debate on whether there is such a thing as a distinct and separate Glasgow sense of humour. You can judge for yourself with these stories from Scotland's biggest city.

WOMEN'S friends can be harsh critics. A reader in a busy Glasgow city centre pub at the weekend heard one woman tell her pal: 'Why did you tell him you were thirty-eight? The last time you saw thirty-eight was waiting for a bus to Shawlands.'

GLASWEGIANS are so romantic, thought a reader from Maryhill catching the bus into town. Two women were discussing the sudden death of a mutual friend's husband. Debating how bad it must be for their friend, one of them opined: 'They were only married fur three year – so she probably still loved him.'

WE once heard a Glasgow chap declare: 'Aye it was rough where I was brought up. If you bought a telly you put the cardboard box in yer neighbour's bin so that it was his hoose they robbed.'

ONLY in Glasgow ... Judy Thomson was watching BBC Reporting Scotland on the arrest in Glasgow connected with a Stockholm terrorist bombing. A neighbour was interviewed about the armed police raid, and said:

'I heard a lot of noise which woke me up. Police were shouting, "Lie down, lie down." Doors were banging, there were firearms.' The neighbour added: 'I thought it must be the end of a party or something.'

MATT Duffy tells us that when he was driving a cab at Anniesland in Glasgow, a little old lady passenger accused taxi drivers of sticking their bottles of Irn-Bru beside the meter as the iron in the drink made the meters go round faster.

'Youse are aw robbers, so ye ur,' she added.

A LAD on Twitter posted a picture of a bag of biscuits with an old sell-by date and stated:

'Tesco selling something nearly two weeks out of date. Not cool.'

Someone from Tesco replied: 'I'm really sorry about that. Can you tell me which store this was in, please?'

But the young chap gave a very Glasgow reply: 'Ah'm no' a grass.'

A READER on the number 9 bus in Glasgow heard an old dear tell her friend that the husband of a mutual friend had just died.

'Was it cancer?' the pal asked.

'No, nothing that serious,' replied the pensioner.

PEOPLE can be a tad harsh at times. A reader in Glasgow heard two women discuss a friend who was struggling to keep her weight under control.

'She's had her stomach stapled,' one confided.

'Stapled to what?' asked her pal. 'Greggs?'

AMERICAN comedian Dave Fulton loves coming to Scotland. But he admitted:

'I was on Bath Street when I asked a local for directions. After he started talking to me, my eyes drifted down to his stomach in the hope that subtitles would appear there.'

WE were reminiscing about the great storm which hit Glasgow in 1968, and David McKenzie told us:

'At three in the morning, slates were crashing from the roof. A neighbour decided to see if his new car was safe. Due to the wind, his wife persuaded him to dig out his old air-raid warden tin hat from the War and wear it for protection.

'The inspection of the car showed it was parked in a sheltered spot, and no damage had occurred. Satisfied, he started to return to his flat when a gust of wind caught the edge of his tin hat, removed it from his head and sent it straight through the windscreen of his new car.'

OUR tall tale of the escaped lion from the former Calderpark Zoo prompts a reader to tell us:

'I was in Easterhouse at the time, and two police officers came running towards me shouting that a lion had escaped.

'"Which way is it headed?" I asked.

'"Are you daft?" one of them replied. "You don't think we're chasing it, do you?"'

'I SAW a guy drop litter,' said the bloke in a Glasgow pub. 'I like my city, so I just picked it up and didn't say anything to him.'

'What was it?' asked his pal.

'A tenner,' he replied.

SOMEONE posted on a website about Glasgow:

'The first day I got into Glasgow, just after catching the bus over from Edinburgh, there was a newspaper poster saying, "Two people stabbed in Glasgow every day".'

We love the comment of someone who replied: 'One of them's probably my mate Kenny. He's always picking stupid fights with bams.'

A FIREFIGHTER swears to us that he had to call round at some pensioners' flats in Glasgow last Halloween to check if the householders had working smoke alarms. One old woman opened the door, saw the uniform and asked if he was not a bit old for that sort of thing as she handed him some sweets.

A READER swears to us he heard a young woman on the bus into Glasgow ask her pal: 'How drunk were you on Saturday?' Then added: 'You were dancing like a woman trying to put on pants four sizes too small with a wasp flying round her head.'

OUR stories of Glasgow's dance halls remind a reader of the classic tale of the chap trying to smuggle a half-bottle under his jacket into the dancing, but just as he approached the door, the bottle slipped and smashed on the pavement.

With the doorman moving menacingly towards him, the chap looks up at the windows above the door and shouts: 'Hey you! That could've killed somebody.'

GLASWEGIANS were determined to give visitors to the Commonwealth Games a good welcome. *Still Game* actor Gavin Mitchell told us:

'Met a nice wee happy guy in Tesco's who told me, "Aye, ah'm across the road in the pub there wi' some English people – ye know The Games' innat. Never tried tablet. Tablet! Imagine that! Cannae huv that. Poor souls." He produced his shopping bag full of it, winked and staggered into the traffic back towards the pub.'

THE Queen's baton for the Commonwealth Games had a successful tour through Scotland. Among the cheering crowds in New Cumnock, Ayrshire, was one local who, observing the entourage that went with the baton, commented:

'We hivnae hud so many polis in the village since the Miners' Strike.'

Incidentally, one police motorcyclist with the baton was asked if they had volunteered for the job. 'Aye, you could say that,' he replied, 'but, in reality, we were voluntelt.'

A READER passing the Rufus T Firefly bar in Hope Street was much taken with the chalk board outside which carried the message: 'To the guy who keeps coming in to do a wee jobby without buying anything, then pretends to be on his phone on the road oot to avoid eye contact – Hiya Pal!'

SO, what's been happening on the streets of Glasgow? A local explained on social media: 'Just seen a drunk woman get knocked down in Glasgow, then two seconds later stand up and shout, "It's awrite – I stayed loose." Is this for real?'

DO you shake your head when you meet people ostentatiously wearing these Fitbits around their wrists that measure the number of steps you take? We pass on the pure daftness of comedy writer Iain Connell, who comments:

'There's a garage in Possil that'll add five hundred miles to your Fitbit for a tenner.'

MEANWHILE in America, the Baltimore weekly newspaper, *City Paper*, carried an article on the similarities between the city and Glasgow. It mentions the film *Braveheart* and memorably explains:

'The movie is a hell of a good time, and, historically, frothing with what in Scotland they call "pish".'

A PARTICK reader swears to us he saw a young lad running along Dumbarton Road wearing a cape so he jocularly shouted after him: 'Are you a superhero?' and the chap shouted back: 'Naw, I've no paid fur ma haircut.'

JUST another weekend in Glasgow. Panto star and comedian Johnny Mac passed on his observation from the city's West End:

'Kelvingrove Park benches – one family enjoying a picnic of hummus and roast vegetables at one, while on another bench a guy is drinking a bottle of Buckfast while on the phone to his mate saying, "No I can't go back to Nicola's flat – I'm just oot some burd's hoose and I've no showered.'"

A VIGNETTE from the streets of Partick on a Friday evening. A woman out running is jogging on the spot at the traffic lights on Dumbarton Road waiting for them to change. A chap in a T-shirt, which appears to be attempting to keep his five bellies under control, is outside the Rosevale Bar having a fag.

'Nice boobs, hen,' he tells the runner, although he might not have used the word boobs.

As the lights change, she replies: 'Likewise, mate,' and heads off as smoker's pal laughs in his face.

WE asked about conversations and events that can only happen in Glasgow. A reader passes on a message he read on social media from a young Celtic supporter who stated:

'One of the guys ah work with is a Rangers fan, but brand new. He had a stroke and was in a coma for a few days. Daft Kev, who's a Celtic fan, sent him a card saying, "Rab you've been in a coma for two years. Celtic got ten in a row! Get it up ye.'"

AS others see us: a magazine in Houston, Texas, the *Houstonia*, started a travel piece about Glasgow last week with the statement: 'Googling Glasgow, the results are sobering. "Pregnant woman attacked and robbed in

Glasgow." "Glasgow gangland wars have scarred city with stabbings, shootings and murder." Scotland's largest city has a bit of a reputation.'

However, the author had a good time when he visited the city, so he then adds the memorable line: 'Don't join a gang, or precipitate a bar fight, and you should be fine.'

WE can just imagine the conversation as young Amna was telling her pals on social media about returning to Glasgow.

Said Amna: 'I was helping out at my dad's shop when a customer asked, "Oh, are ye wan ay the weans?" I replied, "Aye, just helping out for a wee bit the day." Said the customer, "Which wan are ye again? The teacher? Or the wan who never visits?"'

TALES of curmudgeonly café staff reminded Dr Duncan Sim of the service he and a female colleague received in a Bridgeton café. Plonking down two cups of tea, the waitress informed her customers:

'The sugar's in.'

Doc Sim's colleague piped up in protest: 'But I don't take sugar.'

The waitress was not unduly distressed. 'Ach, jist dinnae stir it, hen,' she said and sauntered off.

A WEBSITE offering houses for sale in Scotland hurriedly removed the advertisement for a modern flat in Glasgow's

Southside which declared it was in 'the thieving area of Gorbals'. It returned later rewritten as 'thriving'.

EVEN when celebrating a birthday, Glaswegians can't pass up the chance of a sly wee dig. A Burnside reader on a number 18 bus going through the city's East End spotted a giant poster strung across a wall which declared 'Dougie Robb is fifty today. He cannae believe it.' Underneath was written, 'Neither can we. We thought he was sixty.'

CHART-TOPPING singer-songwriter James Morrison began his latest tour playing to a sell-out crowd in Glasgow's O2 Academy. During his show, he told the audience that he had a special affinity with Glasgow as his nan came from the city.

'She used to give me bags of sweets and tell me, "Go on then, rot your teeth, you wee b*****d,"' he happily recalled.

Yes, you can't beat the warmth of a Glasgow granny.

GLASGOW Lord Provost Liz Cameron, presenting the Freedom of the City to businessman Lord Macfarlane, explained that a member of Lord Macfarlane's family was at the hairdresser before the grand occasion, and when asked by the stylist, in time-honoured tradition, if she was going somewhere nice, explained:

'It's a special occasion. A member of my family is getting the freedom of the city.'

'That's nice,' replied the hairdresser, who then ventured: 'How long was he in for?'

WEST ENDERS parochial? Surely not. It's just that we hear of a chap from Glasgow's West End on a business trip to Beijing, China, who texted his mates to say that he would not be out in the Chip Bar as usual on Friday night as he was 'in the Far East'.

His mate texted back: 'Dennistoun?'

A READER at the panto *Pinocchio* at Glasgow's Pavilion Theatre tells us the fire alarm rang during the performance. The 1,200 audience members dutifully trooped out into the street. They were followed out by the cast in their costumes, which led to one wee Glesga wummin saying to her tot: 'Look, hen, Ah told you it wis real – even the fairy got papped oot!'

A WEST END socialite saw her local dry cleaners had a three-for-two offer on cleaning dresses and took a few along. Unfortunately, the small print said it did not apply to evening dresses, and she and the cleaning assistant got into an argument about what constituted an evening dress. As the assistant said her dresses did not qualify for the special offer our reader indignantly asked how the assistant would define what dresses the offer applied to.

In a convincing example of Glasgow logic, the assistant replied: 'Dresses you would wear to Asda.'

AUTHOR Allan Morrison, reminiscing about Glasgow conductresses, told the tale of the well-dressed woman and her son who were sitting there as the conductress came over for their fares.

'One and a half, conductress,' came a commanding voice.

'Missus,' replied the conductress looking intently at them both. 'That boy o' yours is sixteen if he's a day'.

'I'll have you know I've only been married twelve years,' said the lady.

'Listen, hen,' she replied. 'Ah'm only takin' ferrs – no' confessions.'

NEWS that people are spending less money on home improvements reminds us of the Glasgow council official visiting a house in Blackhill, where he noted that the tenant had knocked through archways in all the rooms so that you could travel from the living room to the kitchen to the bedroom and back round to the living room.

When asked why he had done so, he replied: 'To train my greyhound.'

THE demolition of the Red Road flats in Glasgow reminds Maggie Wood in Australia: 'It wasn't a bad place to live. My mum was in a wheelchair and did her windae hingin' electronically – the concierge camera in the foyer could be accessed via a channel on your telly. Weekend nights were a bit X-rated when amorous lovers didn't realise the glass-fronted foyer didn't offer the same privacy as a back close.'

GOOD to know that certain old Glasgow cinema habits die hard. The Grosvenor Cinema in the West End has put up a message on Facebook: 'Could the owner of this piece of clothing found in screen two last night please put their sheepish hand up?' The picture beneath shows a black bra.

A BIG hit at the Glasgow IMAX cinema was the Batman film, *The Dark Knight Rises*, whose opening scenes were filmed in Scotland. In the queue to go in, one fan told his pal: 'They even filmed some scenes in Glasgow.'

'So, who's the baddy this time? The Yoker?' he replied.

A CLARKSTON reader at Glasgow's Central Station watched a young gum-chewing woman, with her dyed blonde hair harshly scraped back from her face and tied in a bun, walk past two chaps who eyed her up.

After she had passed, one of them told his mate: 'That's what they call a Castlemilk face lift.'

THE Glasgow Art Club in Bath Street hosted an exhibition of paintings by the late James D. Robertson, the inspirational lecturer from Glasgow Art School. The catalogue by Robin Hume includes the story: 'Jimmy treasured an altercation with a lady at one of his summer schools over her use of colour. She had, she insisted, read many books on the subject and was well acquainted with "all the colours of the scrotum".'

A READER who was having a fag outside a Byres Road pub the other night was approached by a mendicant who asked:

'Excuse me, pal, any chance of a fag?'

Our reader not unreasonably pointed out: 'You're already smoking one, mate.'

'Just planning for the future,' the beggar replied.

ONLY in the West End one suspects... our late chum Rony Bridges was standing on Byres Road reading a *Big Issue* he had bought when a woman took it out of his hands and gave him £2. He feels he was perhaps just a tad too casually dressed.

Or as a friend cruelly remarked on his dress sense: 'You been running through Oxfam again? With sticky tape on?'

WE asked for your memories of the Glasgow Garden Festival and Pat Davis recalls:

'As a musician in the 1980s, I had the privilege of knowing some of the most skilled work-dodgers on the planet. One guy, who busked on the violin outside bingo halls, was already in his mid-thirties and had never had a "proper" job.

'As Thatcherism bit, he was called to the dole office regularly, where he insisted that the only suitable position would be as first violinist in a concert orchestra. Then one day the weary dole officer simply smiled and handed him a card with an address where he was told to report.

'I didn't see him for some months before visiting the Garden Festival. On entering the catering hall, I was amazed to see our man, for the first time ever in a suit and black tie, sitting in the front row of the band and sawing his fiddle in a completely scunnered manner, having had to cope with six months of gainful employment.'

AN actor playing a panto baddie in Glasgow says his favourite pantomime joke came in *Robinson Crusoe* at the King's, when Rikki Fulton as the Dame turned to Larry Marshall and declared:

'Jings! Mah feet are killin' me.'

'Whit's wrang wi yer feet?' enquired Larry.

'Sciatica,' said Rikki.

'Hoo can ye ha' sciatica in yer feet?' asked Larry.

'Well, these shoes are size six, an' see ah take a seven.'

ROBERT Murphy, scriptwriter on the Stephen Tompkinson television series *DCI Banks*, knew he was back in Glasgow when he asked a shop assistant what forms of payment he could make.

'We accept,' said the assistant, 'everything apart from American Express, and ginger beer bottles.'

AUTHOR Janice Galloway, appearing at Edinburgh Book Festival, was reminded by event host Ruth Wishart of the advice Janice's granny gave Janice when she was growing up in the Ayrshire seaside resort of Saltcoats. The old lady would warn her: 'Don't go near the Glasgow folk, Janice, they're on their holidays. Anything could happen.'

AMERICAN author Gary Shteyngart was signing copies of his best-selling book *Super Sad True Love Story* at Glasgow's Aye Write! book festival when a fan put in front of him a book already encased in a plastic cover.

Perhaps Gary, who signed the copy with a flourish, thought it was someone who just took good care of his books, but a member of the Mitchell Library where the event had taken place knew better – only in Glasgow surely would someone ask an author to sign a library book.

WE have a vague memory – drink had been taken – of Peter McDougall, who wrote the screenplay for the film of Boyle's book, telling us that a mock-up of a pub was built in the East End of Glasgow to film scenes. A local hard man wandered in and ordered a pint. The actor barman explained it was not a real pub, but a film set. The chap came to the conclusion that the barman was taking the mickey – and decked him.

A READER swears to us he heard a young girl walking down Byres Road in Glasgow ask her pals: 'Do you think I'm vain?' She then added before they could reply: 'It's just that I read in a magazine article that really good-looking people often are.'

FOLK were posting their strange stories about Glasgow on the social media site Reddit with one local reminiscing:
'Saw a guy get punched unconscious in the middle of the road outside a nightclub. Everyone piled around him, wondering what to do, when some lassie breaks through the crowd, saying, "Let us through, ah know furst aid, let us through." She kneels down next to him, unloosening his

laces saying, "Ye awright, pal, ye awright, aye just stay still," and then runs off with his shoes.'

THE Glasgow banter . . . the driver of an early evening bus on Maryhill Road announced to passengers that, because it was quiet, he would perform a guided tour for their illumination.

'They big widden things on your left,' he announced. 'They're trees. The green stuff on the grun is grass.

'See that fire station on your left – that's where pole-dancing started in Glesca.'

Thus ended the brief but educational commentary.

AH, the joys of youth. Ellen Crawford was out walking in Glasgow when a young chap came towards her on a bike. He stopped, pointed to where he had come from, and asked her: 'Are you going that way?'

When Ellen answered in the affirmative, he proudly replied: 'Good – you'll see ma skid.'

2
Scotland the Brave

We must be fair to the rest of Scotland, though, where humour also abounds.

LYNDA Nicolson tells us about a Hamilton colleague whose aunt wrote a Christmas card for a new neighbour, and she addressed it to Mr Candle.

She had been told his name was Mr Connell – but had assumed that was just the local pronunciation.

COMEDIAN Frankie Boyle, at a charity gig in Edinburgh, explained to visitors to the capital that they hadn't seen the real Scotland until they had been to Bathgate.

'I was once on a bus going through Bathgate at night,' he said, 'and I saw a man urinating against a front door – then he opened the door and went in.'

AN English chap working in Glasgow was telling his colleagues in the pub: 'I got a train to Airdrie the other night. The ticket chap said it would be 19:45 when we arrived.

'He was being a bit harsh – it looked more like the early 1960s to me.'

FRANCIS Rossi of Status Quo, on a music site which lists band's worst gigs ever, proposed Dundee in 1969, where he recalled: 'This fight broke out. I'd never seen anything like it – one and a half thousand people, everybody punching everyone else: men punching men, men punching women, women punching men, women punching women – it was like the Wild West.

'Luckily someone told us to get our stuff and get out. We didn't argue, we just left. We came back in the morning and about twenty washerwomen were there in a line, on their knees, scrubbing blood out of the lovely new parquet floor.'

Worst gig? Folk in Dundee would describe it as a great night out.

DERIL Wyles in Stirling revealed: 'Guy from the TV licence chapped my uncle's pal's door who told him he didny have a telly, and the guy was like, "You've got an aerial on your roof."

'He replied: "I've got a pint of milk in the fridge – disny mean I've got a coo out the back," and shut the door.'

THE *National Geographic* in America sent Andrew Evans to visit Barra and he wrote that he asked a shop assistant at Glasgow Airport if she had ever been there. Continued Andrew:

'"Aye!" she surprised me. "I had my first drink in Barra!"

'"So, it was fun then?" I asked, imagining her among a crowd of young people in a dark pub.

'"I was eleven years old," she surprised me again. "I was in the pub wi' my family and the folks there jes' handed me a pint."

'Somehow you never see that on the Visit Scotland advertisements.'

WE pass on the observation from freelance journalist Dayna McAlpine in Edinburgh who spent a few years working in London: 'My pals think living in Scotland is all beautiful rolling hills and friendly patter when in reality it's a junkie shouting, "Ye going' for a s***e, hen?" at me because I'm carrying a sixteen-roll pack of toilet paper.'

NEIL Arthur on Arran tells us that for many years bagpipe tunes were named after battles, or regiments' farewells to trouble spots, such as the 'Barren Rocks of Aden'.

Perhaps a piper's life isn't so exciting anymore, as he noted from the World Pipe Band Championships that Lothian & Borders Police band's medley included 'The Day the Co-op Flooded'.

WE love the sheer poetry of former Communards multi-instrumentalist turned vicar, the Rev Richard Coles, who wrote on social media: 'Whenever I take the Sleeper to Glasgow I wake up and open my window and discover we're behind Iceland in Motherwell, and I watch the rats scampering around and think, "You don't see that on a tin of shortie."'

AN excitable news report in *The Herald* claimed that families travelling to the beach at Troon were 'terrorised by hundreds of drunken youths'. A Glasgow reader tells us:

'Many years ago, I witnessed absolutely disgusting behaviour on Troon beach. I saw a man and woman having an almighty argument in front of loads of kids. Suddenly the woman smacked the chap on the head and it all kicked off. There was a massive brawl and someone called the police. This poor officer turned up on his own and took out his baton to the man. Then the chap snatched the baton and hit the police officer. Then, out of nowhere, a crocodile crept up and stole all the sausages.'

THE esteemed *New York Times* has turned its attention to the bams' dram Buckfast by writing about the tonic wine's association with mindless violence in Scotland. We think Scotland is being a tad slighted here, as it writes:

'The distributors of Buckfast say there is no medical evidence to link their product to such crimes. But the criticism has cast a cloud over this tranquil rural corner of western England, where Buckfast Abbey is an important part of the local economy, and the notion of being lectured about alcohol abuse by Scotland seems jarring, if not downright offensive.'

ON Halloween, a trendy young thing from Glasgow went to work in Larbert in a beautiful vintage 1950s white dress with polka dots, plus red cowboy boots, which she had bought on holiday in America. Going for a drink with colleagues afterwards, she was surprised when the pub manager handed her a bottle of Champagne at the end of the night.

Unbeknownst to her, she had won the bar's Halloween costume prize as Alice in Wonderland.

KEEN environmentalists who want to ensure the most biodegradable form of a funeral can now order caskets made from basketweave material. Reader Frank Eardley saw a hearse going past the other day in Edinburgh with one such coffin and heard a chap beside him declare: 'I can't make my mind up if that's a funeral or a very dull picnic.'

JOHN McCann says that Dundee's relationship with money has often been commented on. He tells us: 'Comedian Emo Philips, when he was at the Fringe a few years ago, told the audience, "I love going to Dundee, spending a £20 note, and watching it ripple through the economy like a donkey swallowed by an anaconda."'

MIKE Fagan saw *Braveheart* in Kilmarnock which began, of course, with the sombre killings of Scots by the English king, Edward Longshanks.

That was before the dramatic fightback, where the Scots under Wallace raise long pikes in front of the charging English cavalry, leading to the slaughter of both horses and riders. There was a massive cheer in the cinema with a chap in the back shouting out: 'Aye, youse lot, this wan's no goin' tae penalties!'

A LANARKSHIRE reader hears a bold lad in his local tell a young woman to whom he was chatting that he was from, 'The US of A.'

Our reader was just thinking that the lad's accent did not sound in the least transatlantic, when the chap then added for clarification: 'The underside of Airdrie.'

OUR tales of laid-back Highlanders remind Alastair Hendry in Greenock of his pal's car breaking down in the west Highlands and it being towed to a local garage for repairs. When the chap asked when it would be ready, the owner thought for some time, then told him: 'Two wee whilies.'

DAVE Martin tells us: 'I remember being in the bar of a Lochgilphead hotel when I heard one local ask another if he could borrow his car as he had some items to move.

'"What's wrong with using your car?" he was asked.

'"I've lost my licence so I don't want to be seen driving it," was the reply.'

A READER claims he was in a party of tourists being shown around a Speyside castle when the guide enthusiastically explained: 'Although the main tower is over four hundred years old, not a stone has been touched, nothing has been altered and nothing replaced in that time.'

'Sounds like the same landlord as me,' a Glaswegian in the party piped up.

MATT Vallance in Ayrshire recalls the late Kilmarnock Sheriff R.N. Levitt speaking at a local St Andrew's dinner. He stated that when he first arrived in Kilmarnock the trades people all lived above their premises. 'Today,' he continued, 'they all live in Troon – above their income.'

SCOTTISH rhyming slang that doesn't travel. Rosy Gillies on Arran tells us her gran was working in an Ayrshire hotel where an English couple were staying before going to a local wedding. When she asked where the wedding was, the English chap replied: 'Some place called the Pineapple – sounds quite posh.'

Rosy's gran felt duty bound to explain to them that it was actually the local chapel where the ceremony was taking place.

THE Pope, arriving in Glasgow, reminded reader Jennifer Wilkie about her father-in-law building a wooden altar for the previous Pope when he visited a hospital near Edinburgh.

After dismantling it, he cut it into ten-inch pieces, varnished them, branded 'Pope John Paul stood here' on them and gave them to charities to auction. Unfortunately, says Jennifer, demand was so high that he had to sneak off to B&Q to buy more wood, and his grandson has now worked out that the wooden altar must have covered about fourteen square miles to accommodate all the pieces.

WHAT about an old Edinburgh Festival joke to mark its beginning, a reader asks. Ninian Fergus reminds us of the Edinburgh chap, asked about the festival, who replied that he hoped to catch Ibsen.

'*Doll's House* or *Hedda Gabler?*' he was asked. 'No, Ibsen Rangers at Easter Road a week on Sunday.'

AYRSHIRE councillor John Reid tells us that a van parked in Cumnock's Main Street the other day did not have its handbrake properly applied and, with no one in it, gradually rolled down the hill and smashed into the Co-op funeral parlour's window.

A passer-by looked at the van embedded in the smashed window and declared: 'Only in Cumnock would someone try to ram raid the funeral parlour.'

JIM Fraser from Elie was in Anstruther behind a fisherman's wife who was paying her gas and electricity bills, and he heard her commenting on how expensive the utilities had become.

As the woman put it: 'They're just like fishermen – if you dinna watch them, they're no long in gettin' on top o' you.'

JANETTE White from Kilmarnock has been reminiscing with other folk from the town on Facebook about the good old days. She tells us: 'Someone recalled when the Mormons went into a notorious part of Kilmarnock and offered to take a crowd of youngsters swimming. This being a rare treat, they jumped at the chance and were duly taken to Kilmarnock Baths.

'A few weeks later, they all received baptism certificates through the post.'

A YOUNG reader taking the bus from Edinburgh to St Andrews watched as a fellow passenger approached the driver when it stopped at Glenrothes bus station and asked if they had reached St Andrews.

The driver confirmed it was in fact Glenrothes, then added in explanation: 'If St Andrews looked like this, no one would visit it.'

ONE reader went really far back when we asked for stories about tenement life when he told us:

'A couple during the terrible Clydebank Blitz hurried from their top-floor tenement flat to go to the air-raid shelter when the sirens went.

When they reached the bottom of the stairs, the wife told her husband: "I'll need to go back up – I've left ma teeth."

'Disabusing her, hubby replied, "It's bombs they're droppin' – no aipples."'

A NEWTON MEARNS reader driving on the A83 stopped at the Rest And Be Thankful viewpoint, where a lone piper was playing a soulful lament, watched by a quiet yet appreciative audience. When he finished he went into his case and brought out a container. Assuming the piper was passing it around for donations, our reader stepped forward, hand outstretched with a pile of coins, only to realise too late that the chap was unscrewing an urn and scattering the ashes of a loved one at the viewpoint.

It was an awkward few moments before our generous reader could slip away.

A TOURIST attraction in Dunblane is the postbox painted gold in memory of Andy Murray's Olympic victory.

Local Rob Mackenzie tells us: 'On a lovely sunny day, I walked to the gold box to post a birthday card to my father. As often is the case, there were a few people queuing to get their picture taken beside it, and as I've done many times, I gave the card to the chap posing so that he could post it to make his picture more authentic.

'This time, though, the chap looked at the address and, a bit confused, told me, "This isn't for me!"'

AN Ayrshire reader tells us: 'Sometimes you forget how proud you can feel to be Scottish.'

He was chatting to a work colleague in England who had been in the Royal Navy for twenty years and he asked him if he had ever seen any action. Adds our reader:

'Totally straight-faced he told me, "The guy next to me went down to gunfire once, that was the closest."

'When I asked where, he told me in the 1980s HMS *London* sailed up the Clyde on a Friday night, and as the crew took to the deck to see the city lights, the sailor next to him was struck on the shoulder by a shot fired by a gang of neds on the embankment with an air rifle.'

3

All in a Day's Work

Some people missed their offices during lockdown. These are some of the tales from working.

THE woman ordering a giant meringue in a Byres Road coffee shop was easily overheard as she told her pal:

'So, I just said to my boss, "There's something I'd like to get off my chest."

'When he asked, "What?" I told him, "Your eyes."'

A GLASGOW chap working for an international company had to attend a staff meeting where a motivational speaker was telling them how they could fulfil their potential.

An air-conditioning unit in the corner was clunking away making a bit of a racket, however, and the speaker finally asked: 'Is that noise annoying you as much as me?'

'No, I think you just edge it,' muttered a voice from the back of the room.

A READER told us about the time he worked in a meat-processing factory when the woman in front of him, who was a bit bulky it has to be said, suddenly dropped a large ham from under her voluminous skirt as she was walking past the gate security staff.

He admired her aplomb as she turned to the staff walking out behind her and shouted: 'Right! Which wan o' youse chucked that at me?'

WE heard about the gas serviceman who arrived at a house in West Lothian with his apprentice and while giving a boiler its winter service, the older fellow was joking with his apprentice that despite the age gap he was still fitter than the youngster. To settle it, he challenged the apprentice to see who could run back to their van faster.

When they did so they were surprised to see the house-holder running after them.

When they asked him why, he told them: 'When I see two gas men running as hard as you two were, I thought I'd better run, too.'

WORKPLACE nicknames. A reader tells us: 'I remember my father talking about a foreman at Babcocks who was known as The Sheriff as he was often heard asking, "Where's the hold up?"'

Joe Hunter tells us: 'A foreman in the shipyards was known as The Balloon as he was forever telling the workers, "Don't let me down."'

DOUG King recalls an old colleague whose secretary brought him a letter to sign. Sadly, she had, by mistake, typed the town of Biggar as Buggar. He attached a note stating 'Make Buggar Biggar' and passed it back. Of course, inevitably, the redraft came back with Buggar in a larger type.

AYR artist Sandra Ratcliffe, en route to Gigha for an exhibition of her paintings, was stuck in the lift of her block of flats with many of her canvasses.

She shouted for help, and neighbours called the fire brigade.

The firefighter who prised the lift doors open, looked at all the paintings surrounding her and remarked: 'Just how long have you been in here?'

AN Ardrossan reader told the tale of the minister who regularly was shaved by the local barber, a member of his flock. Unfortunately, the barber had the previous evening imbibed rather too well of the juice of the barley and, despite concentrating, his trembling hand caused him to nick the minister's cheek and draw blood.

'That's the whisky that causes that,' said the minister solemnly.

'That's right,' replied the barber. 'It does make your skin a hell of a tender.'

DEBBIE Meehan told us of a friend having her nails manicured who was asked by the beautician what she did for a living.

'I'm an anaesthetist,' she replied.

'What's that?' said the beautician.

'I put people to sleep,' she explained in simple terms.

'Oh, is that not very sad?' said the girl.

THREE loud office workers having a drink after work on Friday in Glasgow were en route to their staff Christmas party when one was asked if she would kiss her boss under the mistletoe.

'I wouldn't even kiss him under anaesthetic,' she replied.

A READER in Glasgow tells us an office colleague announced the other day: 'I have a cold shower every morning.'

Everyone was thinking how hardy that must be when the chap added: 'Right after my wife and daughters have finally finished having hot ones.'

ENTERTAINER Andy Cameron told us the classic Glasgow shipyard tale:

'Jimmy McCrindle, aka The Pig, was a legend in Govan. The gaffer was passing him one day and enquired, "Is that whisky ah can smell off your breath, McCrindle?"

'The Pig replies, "It better be, or that licensed grocer on Govan Road is gettin' a doin'."'

ONE ageing boss admitted to us that he was persuaded by younger staff to attend a trendy nightspot after their office Christmas party where the doorman stopped him and said:

'Sorry, bud. You've had too many.'

'What, drinks?' asked the boss.

'No, birthdays,' said the steward.

AH yes, the office Christmas parties. One Glasgow worker once told us: 'At our office do we could bring our partners, so my wife met many of my co-workers for the first time. I can now tell how attractive the women in my office are by the number of times my wife told me an individual looked like a tramp.'

We also liked the story of the girl who arrived at her office Christmas party straight from a session in a tanning salon.

Worried that the goggles had left a white ring around her eyes she asked her pal:

'Do I look like a clown?'

'Put it this way, Sophie,' her pal replied. 'Ah wouldnae be surprised if weans start askin' ye fur balloons.'

THE Hilton Hotel in Glasgow had a birthday bash with guests entertained by local nine-piece soul band Counselled Out. Lead vocalist Drew Robertson broke off from introducing the next number to tell his audience: 'Please refrain from taking pictures of the band for security reasons.'

A few folk nodded their heads in sympathy with the added problems that life brings these days, when Drew added, after looking at his fellow band members: 'Social security reasons.'

SO why should women know much about car mechanics? We only ask as a worker at Glasgow's most famous chain of car showrooms tells us a woman customer was having her car repaired only to be told by the wee Glasgow mechanic: 'Yer heid gasket's blew.'

She then asked him: 'What colour should it be?'

THE head of a company's human resources department swears to us a chap was asked at a job interview the standard question:

'What do you think is your greatest weakness?'

'Honesty,' he replied.

'I don't think honesty is a weakness,' he was told.

'I don't give a toss what you think,' he responded.

A GLASGOW office worker tells us a young Polish woman from one of Poland's oldest cities has joined the team, and is putting everyone to shame by always being the first to arrive every morning. She's told everyone that her nickname is Krakow Dawn.

A BEARSDEN reader tells us his neighbour, who is a doctor, felt a warm glow when he was driving his young daughter to school and she picked up his stethoscope and put it in her ears. Just as he was thinking it was a sign she also wanted to enter the medical profession, she spoke into it: 'Welcome to McDonald's. May I take your order?'

A MILNGAVIE reader tells us she was having some work done in the garden when one of the gardeners knocked on the door and asked if he could use the toilet. As she had just washed the kitchen floor, and seeing the state of his boots, she told him:

'I'll just put some newspapers down.'

'I'd rather use the toilet,' he replied.

A GLASGOW reader tells us she was moving office and had to clear out her desk, which is why she staggered off her train home with a large black bin bag in each hand, full of her office bits and pieces. Her mood wasn't helped when she walked past the local pub and a smoker outside remarked:

'Good lord, missus. What size of dug do you have?'

A READER reminiscing about the changes in his job over the years tells us: 'If I could tell my twelve-year-old self that my job in the future would involve using passwords every day, I fear he would think it was going to be a lot more exciting than it actually is.'

CAMERON Thomson in Strathaven confessed to us:

'When I was a young teller in a bank in Larkhall I was more than a little zealous when applying the rules. I was approached by a local worthy, who wanted £10 from his savings account, and I insisted on asking for ID. This prompted the gentleman to turn to his pal in the queue behind him and say, "Tell this wean who ahm ur," which brought a confirmation announcement of, "Aye, it's him."

'ID process complete, he got his tenner.'

A GLASGOW reader swears to us he was in a city pub when a younger chap came in and told his pals he had lost his new job as a waiter. When his mates asked what happened he told them: 'The boss asked me if I could clear table five. I told him I hadn't tried the high jump since school, but I would give it a go.'

TOM Strang in Barrhead recalled his student days driving a van for Ascot Bakery in Greenock.

Says Tom: 'As the last customer left my van, a four-year-old boy jumped into the back and said, "Mister, gies a bun."

'When I asked if he had any money and he said no, I told him he couldn't have one. After a five-second delay, the urchin said, "Gies a bun, mister, or I'll fart in your van."

'He duly got the bun.'

A STRUCTURAL engineer from south of the Border, newly arrived in Glasgow, was struggling to persuade local workmen to remove material from a site. After ranting at length, he demanded to know when, precisely, the material would be shifted. The bored foreman answered:

'Ah've no' got a scooby, pal.'

To which the exasperated chap pleaded: 'Well, go get one. Hire a Scooby if you have to. Just get this stuff removed.'

STAFF at a Glasgow office were dragooned into a meeting room for a talk by an inspirational speaker hired by the company for some reason. When the speaker asked: 'What inspires you to get up every day?' someone in the audience answered: 'My bladder mostly.'

A GLASGOW reader tells us his pal is known for his funny stories and told him the other day: 'My boss emailed me and said he was having to give a speech and could I tell him some jokes. I emailed him back and said I was very busy working, but would send him something later. He emailed me back saying, "That's hilarious. Send some more."'

TALES of taking your own food into work reminded John Milligan: 'As a young fireman in the 1970s, when acting as kitchen assistant to an older, worldly-wise fireman in

Kilmarnock Fire Station, the cook discovered he was one fish short for a fish and chips lunch. It didn't take long for him to stave off a potential mutiny. He produced a piece of white bread, cut off the crusts and shaped it to look like a fish fillet. With breadcrumbs applied it was deep fried along with the others and put out for lunch. The strange thing was, there were no complaints.'

OUR mention of firefighters cooking meals for their crew reminded one retired fireman: 'Assisting the cook, I dropped an egg which broke under the kitchen table. Apologising to him, I said I'd put it in the bin, but he said he could still use it. I pointed out that the egg was now actually full of small bits of dirt and grit but he said it'll be okay as they'll just think it's pepper. We used the egg without any complaints.'

HOT weather reminds us of the Glasgow girl at a job interview on a hot day who walked in and remarked: 'S'awfy clammie!' The English chap conducting the interview replied: 'Please take a seat, Sophie.'

And the toper in the Glasgow pub who felt brave enough to tell his pals: 'I was so hot in bed last night I had to cuddle up to the wife to get cold.'

A READER tells us about an office night out at a comedy club where quite a reserved chap made the mistake of going to the loo during the main turn, only to be verbally lacerated from the stage. The heat from his face, apparently, could have powered a three-bar fire.

Our reader was then amazed when another chap stood up and walked to the loo, only to be bawled at by the turn: 'Where are you going?'

But in a Glasgow accent he gruffly replied: 'I'm going for a pee before the comedian comes on,' which left a deafening silence from the stage.

KEITH Murray tells us about a relative working for Scottish Power who asked a caller for his postcode. That is, after all, usually enough to identify where the caller lives. This time, though, the postcode did not show up on the computer, so she then asked:

'Do you have a street name?'

'Aye, well, ma pals call me "The Iceman" sometimes,' he replied.

THE young woman ordering the large white wine on a Friday took a large gulp before telling her pal:

'That idiot boss of mine said I would get a pay rise when I earned it.' After another slurp she added: 'If he thinks I'm going to wait that long, he's got another think coming.'

WITH all the interest in the history of the Clyde, Jim McDonald in Carluke remembers when he started as an apprentice at Fairfield Shipbuilders, in Govan, and was soon challenged by his journeyman to take part in the annual race between journeymen and the apprentices, from Govan Cross to Shieldhall.

Knowing how fit the apprentices were, he asked what the catch was, but was told there was no catch – all the journeymen wanted was three yards of a start.

It was a while before the penny dropped that the three yards the journeymen had in mind were Harland & Wolff, Fairfields and Alexander Stephen and Sons.

A READER tells us he was in the office communal kitchen where he saw a bag with 'Spat on' written on the side. He was telling a colleague how disgusting he thought that was, but was greeted with a mystified look.

So, he pointed again at what was written, until his colleague told him: 'That's Sadie Paton's.'

SO, do we believe the reader who claimed he was on a bus and heard the chap in front tell the female with him that he had just got a job in a bowling alley?

'Tenpin?' she asked him.

'No, it's a permanent position,' he replied.

BILL Moore tells us: 'I knew a Glasgow guy who was being interviewed for a general handyman job at McGill University in Montreal. He desperately wanted the job, and the last question in the interview was:

'"Tell us, Mr Gallagher, can you do cement work?"

'"Can Ah dae cement work?" he replied. "Did they find Jimmy Hoffa?"

Adds Bill: 'He got the job.'

A LABOUR politician campaigning to save shipyard jobs at Govan Cross was beckoned over by an elderly Govanite. The old boy said that in the 1970s his wife had anxiously asked union leader Jimmy Reid if any shipyard workers were to be laid off as she was worried about her man's job.

Jimmy told her: 'We're fighting for every man, Mary, but it looks like six fitters are being made redundant.'

'That's all right,' said Mary. 'My husband's only five foot six.'

A READER couldn't help smiling when he was at a business reception in Edinburgh and watched a chap go up to an American woman with the name 'Twila' on her badge and say: 'That's a name you don't hear every day.'

'Actually, I do,' she coolly replied.

WE reminisced about the boozy business lunches of old and John Gilligan tells us of Big John who covered the Southside of Glasgow for Dryburghs the brewers in the late 1960s. He recalls: 'One day John was accompanied by a senior manager from England who, after his eighth call to licensed premises, and the eighth alcoholic beverage, asked John:

"'Do you always drink this much during the day?"

'Big John replied, "Naw, some days we go fur a bevy."'

A READER tells us a young girl in her office was enthusiastic about having a dolphin tattooed on her bottom, but seemed a bit down afterwards.

When our reader gently enquired why, the girl blurted out: 'When he'd finished he asked me if I wanted anything else done, as there was plenty of room left.'

SHIPYARD tales remind us of the pay negotiations at the old John Brown's yard where a shop steward declared: 'Ah've tellt ye . . . nae mair moolah, the bears are oot!'

An American executive turned to a local colleague for elucidation, only to be told: 'Basically, he's sayin' the ba's on the slates.'

'MY wife always likes to put on a happy face,' said the chap in the pub the other night. 'Which might explain why she got sacked from the make-up counter at a department store.'

THE news that the government-owned Royal Bank of Scotland is to sack workers in Scotland and transfer their jobs to India reminds Fraser Kelly in Singapore of the classic yarn of the Kelvinside lady who tries to phone her local bank branch but is put through to an Indian call centre.

She insists: 'I want to talk to Mary in my local branch,' but the chap who answered doggedly tells her: 'Madam, I have two degrees and have been superbly trained by the RBS. I can do anything for you that this Mary can.'

'I don't think so,' she tells him.

But he stands his ground: 'Madam, I have the finest IT system here and can tell you anything faster than any branch person in Scotland can.'

'Okay,' she finally relents. 'Did I leave my gloves on the branch counter this morning?'

THE Royal Bank's decision to sack Scottish workers and move jobs to India also reminds Ian MacLean of when he worked at Lloyds TSB and a customer phoned the bank's call centre in India to say she had lost her husband and needed information about their joint account.

The polite call-centre worker dutifully answered her query, and earnestly ended the call by hoping that she found her husband soon.

WE hear of the computer repair shop in Glasgow which had difficulty with its support staff phoning customers to offer them a software update.

It seems that phoning folk and saying: 'Ahm gonnae come roon and put your Windows in,' wasn't regarded as all that welcoming.

LUNCHTIME drinking is of course a thing of the past for most workers these days.

One retired boss in Glasgow tells us a few of his younger staff were drinking vodka at lunchtime so that their breath wouldn't smell of alcohol.

He told them that he would prefer it if they drank whisky, as he thought it would be better if the customers thought they were drunk rather than just stupid.

'A LARGE roll of bubble wrap arrived in the office and I asked the boss what to do with it,' said the young office assistant.

He said, 'Just pop it in the corner.'

'Took me two hours.'

A GLASGOW businessman tells us that writing negative references for former employees is no longer allowed at his company, for fear of being sued.

He felt, though, that he had got round the problem when he was asked for his opinion on a worker who constantly skived off before being shown the door. 'A man like him is hard to find,' he eventually stated.

STORIES of ambiguous references lead to Ian Hutchison remarking: 'I was reminded of the one which I have always enjoyed. "He came fired with enthusiasm, and that is how he went."'

REFERENCES continued. Celia Stevenson tells us: 'I have an American friend who, if he has to give a reference for a less than satisfactory employee, writes, "If you can get X to work for your company, you will indeed be fortunate."'

A COLLECTION of writings by the legendary *Herald* editor Arnold Kemp was published entitled, 'Confusion to Our Enemies'. Although folk remember him as a statesman-like editor, he was far cheekier in his younger days. As a young journalist on the *Scotsman*, he and some colleagues spooked the night news editor with a fake wire story sent down the tubes saying that a flying saucer had landed at Buckingham Palace.

Much to their consternation, the night editor cleared the front page for the story. Fearing it would lead to their sacking, Arnold stopped him by then sending a fake D Notice from the government stating that the story had to be kept secret.

v sweets	
Chocolate Fudge Cake	3.25
Sticky Toffee Pudding	3.25
Daily Grumble	3.25
Ice Cream	1.95
ft tea/coffee	
Teas	1.50
Latte (for god's sake get a grip)	11.95
Coffee Black or White	1.95
Cappuccino	2.00
Espresso	1.60

The Griffin Bar 266 Bath St Glasgow G2 4JP 0141 331 5

A MILNGAVIE reader swears that he had a handyman fixing some loose tiles on his roof who came down from his ladder and said he would have to go home early as he was feeling a bit dizzy.

'Vertigo?' asked our reader.

'No, not far from the town centre,' replied the handyman.

PROVING that Edinburgh folk really are friendly, Denise Percival tells us a colleague arrived at an Edinburgh law firm and asked the receptionist where the gents' toilet was. 'I'll just come and point you in the right direction,' she replied.

'No need to go that far,' replied her anxious colleague.

JOHN Quinn in Lenzie tells us the true story of a relative with the job of delivery driver for an Indian takeaway, but fed up with the complaints. It came to a head when he returned to the shop and had to speak to a customer saying his crispy poppadoms were broken when they arrived. John's relative said: 'Whit 'ye greetin' aboot? Ye cannae get a whole wan in yer mooth anyhow.'

TOURING Scotland was Italia 'n' Caledonia by Mike Maran and Philip Contini, which tells the story of the many Italians who left sunny hillsides and emigrated to Scotland at the start of last century.

Mike tells us that the people of Lucca in Tuscany were famous for making wax figurines. Seven young statue makers sought their fortune in Scotland and brought a thousand little statues of the Virgin Mary all the way to Paisley – where they didn't sell.

Anyway, one of the seven, a chap called Nardini, bought the statues from his six companions who returned to Italy. Nardini set to work and converted the thousand Marys into a thousand Santa Clauses, sold the lot, and opened a café in Largs with the profits.

JOB application forms: a North Kelvinside reader tells us he was very tempted, when he reached the box which asked 'Salary expected' to write in it 'Friday'.

WE felt for the guy in the West End bar at the weekend who was asked by a comely young woman:

'You look really familiar – what do you do?'

'I'm an actor and a musician,' he modestly told her.

She stared at him a bit longer before adding: 'No, that's not it. Do you work in Sainsbury's?'

'Well, that as well,' he muttered.

A CHAP was in his work canteen in Livingston when the woman serving was complaining to her fellow worker that the flesh on her upper arm had lost its muscle tone.

Despite the queue of folk waiting she jiggled her arm and announced: 'I'm thinking of getting a Saltire tattooed on it – then it would look like it was flapping in the wind.'

THE generation gap in offices comes to mind as we hear of a boss in a Glasgow office who asked a young member of staff to find him a bulldog clip. The youngster emailed him a YouTube video of one wearing a Union flag bowler hat.

CONCERN in the queue at Auchterarder Post Office where customers notice that a member of staff had scrawled 'F. Off' across the office calendar behind the desk. Had someone succumbed to the pressures of the job? Eventually a customer asked what was going on, and was relieved to hear that Fiona had merely marked down an upcoming holiday.

A READER reminds us of the Miners' Strike when picketing miners built a beautiful snowman at their picket line which was destroyed when a police van reversed into it.

The next day the snowman was rebuilt but with a fake police helmet on its head. This appeared to annoy a police driver who then deliberately drove into it. The snag was the miners had rebuilt it over a metal traffic bollard.

SHIPYARD painter Bob Starrett, who chronicled the UCS work-in with cartoons which were later published, once told the story of Wee Bunty the shipyard worker and her team who had sneaked in a half-bottle of whisky to their work. When it was finished she asked one of the painters to fill the empty bottle with turps.

Wee Bunty carefully replaced the cork, went back to the off-licence, innocently explained that it smelled a bit off to her, and when the assistant reeled back from smelling it, he promptly replaced it with a fresh half-bottle.

4

Wedded Bliss

Even the crusty Winston Churchill said his most brilliant achievement was persuading his wife to marry him. But that doesn't mean you can't have a laugh about it either.

A WEST END woman returning from a company party with her husband asked him:

'Have I ever told you how handsome and sexy and totally irresistible to all women you are?'

'Why, no,' replied her deeply flattered husband.

'Then what,' she added, 'gave you that stupid idea at the party?'

A READER swears to us that he was in his local in Glasgow when a woman of a certain age came in to meet her pal who remarked: 'That's a lovely coat.'

'Thank you,' said her pal. 'My husband got it for my forti-eth birthday.'

'Well, it's certainly worn very well,' her pal replied.

AN Ayrshire golf club member confessed he was not really paying attention when his wife returned from a shopping trip to Glasgow and announced that she had bought a new dress. He glanced up from watching the Masters on the telly and said, 'I like the zip down the front. Very sexy.'

His wife shouted back, 'That's the garment bag it's in you idiot.'

A CUMBERNAULD reader heard a chap in the pub moan: 'I thought I was being funny when I told the wife how I was looking forward to her birthday next month as I had never made love to a forty-year-old. She brought me back down to earth when she pointed out that I hadn't made love to a thirty-nine-year-old either.'

A CLYDEBANK reader said he was a neutral observer when his wife and his twenty-something daughter, who still lives at home, began bickering about the young lady being overly picky about boyfriends. He felt he had to say something, though, when the discussion got so heated that his wife declared: 'It's just daft to think you can wait around for the perfect Mr Right. I didn't.'

DO we believe the tale of the married couple out for dinner when the wife asked why her husband kept on looking over at the woman in the drunken stupor at the next table?

'It's my ex-wife,' replied the husband. 'She's been drinking like that since I left seven years ago.'

'Unbelievable,' replied his new spouse. 'I wouldn't think anybody could celebrate that long.'

'ON reflection,' said the chap in the pub the other night, 'when my wife proudly said she could get into the same skirts from before she was married, I shouldn't have replied, "I wish I could."'

A READER was at a drinks reception when a woman tapped a chap on his shoulder and said: 'Hello.' When he turned round, she looked puzzled and blurted out: 'Oh, sorry. You're not the man I thought you were.'

'My wife says that all the time,' he told her.

THE woman having an after-shopping spritzer with her pal in All Bar One in Glasgow was discussing her wedding plans, and whether she should have something meaningful engraved on the inside of her future husband's wedding ring.

'How about "Put it back on",' suggested her pal.

'WOMEN – so hard to please,' said the chap in the East End boozer at the weekend. 'Valentine's night, booked a table for me and the missus for eight o'clock,' he told his pal.

'But her face was still tripping her. I swear it was half eight before she'd even potted her first red.'

'HE'S so tight-fisted,' declared the chap in the Glasgow pub the other night, discussing a mutual friend, 'that if he came home early and saw a plumber's van outside his house, he'd hope his wife was having an affair.'

'EVERY morning,' said the loudmouth in the pub the other night, 'the newly-wed guy next door kisses his young wife goodbye on the doorstep before going to work.

'"So," my wife says to me, "Why don't you do that?"

'"I wouldn't mind," I told her. "But I hardly know the woman."'

A READER was having her hair done in a Glasgow salon. The woman at the next seat was complaining to her hairdresser about her husband's lack of care and attention. Eventually the woman said to her hairdresser:

'Do you think I should divorce him?'

The hairdresser thought about this before replying: 'Oh, I think you should consult at least two hairdressers before taking a decision on that.'

AN East Kilbride reader says he was sitting at home watching the telly when he heard his wife, in the kitchen, ask: 'What would you like for dinner, my sweetheart? Chicken, tuna or lamb?'

Cheered by that, he shouted back: 'Lamb would be great.'

But his wife replied: 'You're having soup. I was talking to the cat.'

THE joker in the pub the other night claimed: 'The wife asked what I was doing on the computer and I said I was looking for cheap flights.'

He added: 'She got all excited, which is strange, as she's never shown any interest in darts before.'

'THE wife and I were talking about making wills,' said the chap in the pub. 'I told her I would leave everything to her.'

He added: 'She told me, "You already do, you lazy so-and-so."'

JOHN Park hears a bemused chap in the pub look at his mobile phone and announce: 'I've just received a blank text from my wife.'

'Is she still not talking to you?' asked his mate.

NOSTALGIA alert! Our mention of the sex and bondage novel *Fifty Shades of Grey* reminds Jim Hair of the gag by the great variety hall comedian Lex McLean who told his Glasgow Pavilion audience:

'Told the wife that black underwear turned me on. So, she didn't wash my vest for a month.'

CHAP in a Glasgow pub swore his wife was insistent when he did the shopping that he buy only organic vegetables.

He said he asked the assistant: 'I'm buying vegetables for the wife. Have they been sprayed with poisonous chemicals?'

'No sir,' the assistant replied. 'You have to do that yourself.'

A GLASGOW woman is heard telling her pals: 'My husband took me out for dinner on our anniversary. I tried to get him to be all romantic during the meal and I asked him to tell me something that would make my heart beat faster.

'So, he told me he'd forgotten to bring his credit card.'

WE bump into a misogynist in a Glasgow pub who declares: 'We had friends round for dinner the other night, and the wife called me into the kitchen and told me to prepare the table.

'So, I went into the dining room and explained to our guests about her cooking.'

A READER asked a pal in a Glasgow pub the other night how it was going with him and his wife both being on a joint diet. 'She's finding it heavy going,' he replied, then added: 'Put it this way. It'd probably be safer for me to go home smelling of perfume than her catching a whiff of a Mars bar from me.'

OUT at a Glasgow pub, a reader heard a young toper tell his pals: 'My wife was at a girlie night out at the Corinthian and said some guy bought her drinks all night, then asked if I was jealous. I told her, "Absolutely. I wish someone would buy me drinks all night."'

A MILNGAVIE reader swears to us he saw a friend leaving the local florist's shop with a plant. When he asked him who it was for, he replied: 'The wife. We had a bit of an argument – but not a huge dozen red roses type of argument.'

A READER in Partick goes all philosophical as he emails: 'The human brain starts working the moment you're born, and never stops until your wife asks where you were last night.'

MARRIED life continued. A chap in a Glasgow golf club tells his mates: 'Every Saturday night I watch *Strictly Come Dancing* with the wife. She turned to me on Saturday and asked me who I wanted to win. Although I've watched it every week, I couldn't name a single person who was on it.'

INTERESTING how married life develops. A reader tells us a chap at his Ayrshire golf club was explaining to fellow members: 'The first time my wife left me for a few days to visit the grandchildren down south, she left me meals she had prepared in the freezer with dates on them explaining when I should eat them. This week when she went all I got was a list of recorded TV programmes that I was instructed not to watch until she got home.'

HEARING a loud yell, Lisa Buchan from Falkirk ran into the kitchen, where her husband told her he thought he had spotted a cockroach. Hubby proceeded to spray everything down while giving all the surfaces a thorough clean.

'If I ever find that cockroach,' says Lisa, 'I'm putting it in the bathroom next.'

THE state of marriages was being discussed in a Glasgow pub the other night where one regular claimed his wife had divorced him because of arithmetic. As this just left everyone puzzled, he was asked to elucidate.

'She put two and two together,' he told them.

A READER swears to us that she was at a seminar on relationships when the speaker urged the women to text their husbands to tell them they loved them.

One woman got a reply asking if she had crashed the car and another was told: 'I thought we agreed afternoon drinking was a bad idea.'

IT was at the wedding of an optician that the minister couldn't resist saying to the couple when they were taking their vows: 'Do you, Karen, take David the optician to be your lawfully wedded husband, for better or worse? Better ... or worse? Better ... or worse?'

A STUDENT working evenings in a Glasgow call centre told us that when he asked one caller about her marital status, she replied: 'I guess we're as happy as any couple these days.'

AND do we believe the reader who claims he overheard a woman in a bar tell her female pals that she and her husband usually ended up in the doggie position in bed. While her friends stared at her she then added:

'Yes, hubby sits up and begs. And I roll over and play dead.'

WE are told that a Whitecraigs lady went into her local newsagent's to pay for her newspapers being delivered and explained that, as she had recently become divorced, she was reverting to her maiden name.

'Is the address still the same?' asked the assistant.

'Yes,' replied the customer.

'Still, you managed to keep the house then?' replied the assistant.

A LANARKSHIRE girl on holiday in India with her boyfriend phoned her parents in great excitement the other day to say that her boyfriend had got down on one knee and proposed to her outside the Taj Mahal, arguably the most romantic building in the world.

'What a coincidence,' her dad told her. 'Me and your mum met outside the Pir Mahal in Hamilton.'

A READER having coffee in Glasgow's city centre heard the woman at the next table bemoaning to friends that the daughter of a fellow friend was, in her opinion, too young to get married.

When her friends argued that perhaps she was old enough, the first woman argued: 'They've got a PlayStation on their wedding list, for goodness' sake.'

A CASE at Greenock Sheriff Court involved an affray in a local restaurant. A diner who appeared as a witness was asked by the fiscal:

'Were you there on a date?'

'No,' the chap replied. 'I was with the wife.'

A FALKIRK reader heard a female stopping a pal in the High Street and telling her:

'Did you hear that Margaret's just had her second husband cremated?'

'Aye, Ah know,' replied her pal. 'Some of us cannae find a husband, and others have husbands to burn.'

SOMEONE not winning any gallantry awards was the best man at a wedding who telephoned the office which produced a road safety poster plastered on the rear of Edinburgh buses.

The caller explained that the poster featured a street scene containing the bride's house. He asked if he could get a copy of the poster, then added: 'I want to say in my speech that every time I see the bride she always reminds me of the back of a bus!'

RETURNING home in the evening rush hour to Helensburgh, a reader heard a chap on the train tell a pal: 'The wife tells me I snore when I'm sleeping. But that's rubbish. No one at work has ever mentioned it.'

A KILMAURS reader hopes the customer in front of him at the check-out at Marks & Spencer was joking when she was offered a gent's tie for only a penny by the assistant. It was part of a promotion by the store to mark its 125th anniversary.

The woman took the tie and told the assistant: 'It'll do for his Christmas while I'm away on my Caribbean cruise.'

STEVEN Elder writes in: 'My wife left a note on the fridge. It said: "This isn't working anymore. I'm at the end of my tether. I'm away to stay at my mother's."

'I opened the fridge. The light came on and the beer was cold. Nothing wrong with the fridge. Nae idea what she's on about.'

GALES of laughter in a West End bar recently when a group of women were discussing what they had in common with their husbands. One of the ladies was a bit stumped until all she could finally come out with was: 'We got married on the same day.'

A GLASGOW chap in the pub at the weekend was claiming his wife was incredibly jealous as she found a long blonde hair on his jacket and accused him of having an affair.

'That's nothing,' said his mate. 'My wife found no hair on my jacket – and accused me of cheating on her with a bald woman.'

STUART Miller tells us of a wedding in one of Scotland's more magnificent churches where the staff announced that there had been a mix-up, the organist had been double-booked and couldn't come, but there was a piano if anyone could play it.

Eventually the couple went up the aisle to an older woman amongst the guests who could play the only religious song she knew, 'Stand Up, Stand Up for Jesus', with two fingers.

'The magnificence was muted,' says Stuart.

A YOUNG lady phones to tell us how to work out if you are posher than royal bride Kate Middleton.

The formula apparently is to multiply your weekly glasses of wine by the number of Apple products you own, then subtract your total number of tattoos multiplied by the number of missing teeth.

JIM Grier in Saltcoats tells us about a recent wedding in Ayrshire where the nervous bride, struggling to keep a steady hand while signing the register, was advised by the minister that it might help if she put her weight on it. After the ceremony the minister noticed that after her signature she had added, '8st 7lb'.

FAVOURITE Twitter message we've read this week: 'My husband complains I put too much information on Twitter. Clearly, his haemorrhoids are making him cranky.'

WE asked for your Scottish wedding tales. Gavin Paterson recounts: 'Playing in a wedding band for over twenty-five years, I remember being on stage in an East End of Glasgow hall when a huge fight broke out on the dance floor.

'Word had spread that the best man had been caught in an intimate moment with the newly married bride.

'The father of the bride came to the microphone to quell the fight by announcing, "Right stop the fighting. The best man has apologised." It worked too.'

A HYNDLAND reader tells us his wife announced that, to try to give herself an incentive to lose weight, she would treat herself to a new pair of shoes for every ten pounds she lost.

He now realises that replying: 'That's a lot of new shoes,' wasn't the encouragement she was looking for.

'I'M worried that the wife is losing her mind,' said the chap in the golf club bar the other night. 'She keeps on telling me that she's talking to a brick wall.'

A CHAP in the pub the other night declared: 'The wife says we would have less arguments if I wasn't so pedantic.'

He added: 'So I told her that surely she meant "fewer".'

THE desultory conversation in a Glasgow bar at the weekend was enlivened by one chap declaring: 'The wife had a funny dream last night. She dreamed she'd married a millionnaire.'

'You're lucky,' said a customer further up the bar. 'Mine dreams that in the daytime.'

THE chap in the Glasgow pub at the weekend was being less than chivalrous when he announced: 'The wife tells folk that twenty years after she got married, she still fits her wedding dress. What she doesn't tell them is that she was seven months pregnant at the time.'

A READER claims he heard a woman in Glasgow tell her pals her local jeweller's had a necklace in the sales at a great price. They asked if she bought it and she told them: 'I put a deposit down and they said they would hold on to it until my husband did something unforgivable.'

WE don't get many *Big Issue* stories these days as it has now become less remarkable to see people selling it. However, a reader swears to us that he heard a business chap being asked:

'Would you like a *Big Issue* pal?'

He replied: 'No thanks. I'm sure my wife will already have one lined up for me when I get home.'

A WEST END woman tells us: 'I had a woman's voice on my car's GPS giving me instructions on how to get to places, but then I discovered I could change it to a man's voice. I switched it over to the man, but all it ever said was, "It's around here somewhere. Just keep driving."'

5

Broadening the Mind

And, of course, away from the office the fun continues when holiday season arrives.

WE were reminded of the elderly mum from Glasgow visiting her son in America and being asked on arrival at United States immigration: 'Ma'am, do you have any meats, fruits or any other foodstuffs with you?'

'Aw, son,' she replied sympathetically. 'Ah huvny even a sweetie ah can gie ye.'

A BEARSDEN reader holidaying on Lanzarote tells us a little boy aged about six came running up the beach to tell his sunbathing mother in a distinctly Glasgow accent: 'A big wave knocked me over and a wummin had tae help me oot.'

'What was yer da doin?' asked the mum.

'Laughin," replied the wee boy.

AHEAD of Fair Friday, a Kelvinside reader recalled being at the Bobby Jones dance hall in Ayr many moons ago in his youth when a young Glasgow girl on holiday during the Fair was being enthusiastically 'winched' at the side of a hall by a fellow holidaymaker.

The girl drew herself away from the clinch to tell the chap: 'If yer lookin' fur ma tonsils, they were removed when I was eight.'

THE announcement that the *Buteman* newspaper is to close reminds us of the story from the paper of the countryside ranger who went to check an eight-foot-long bird hide at Ascog Loch which had been built to help twitchers spot the rare birds that stop off on Bute on their annual migrations.

Inside, he found a family of four from Glasgow who were having a holiday in it, complete with food, milk, newspapers and a fold-up settee.

A READER on holiday in Torremolinos in Spain heard a Scottish youth in a bar say to a young woman:

'I bet I can talk you into taking off your T-shirt.' The young woman sneeringly dismissed his wager as extremely unlikely.

At that, the young lad added: 'I've just seen a spider crawl inside it.'

A GLASGOW reader swears to us that he was on a Ryanair flight to Spain alongside a group of boisterous lads on a stag weekend. One of the chaps had a seat beside a young woman whom he tried to engage in conversation with the line:

'Do Ryanair charge you extra to sit beside a handsome young man?'

'Yes, they do,' she immediately responded. 'But I wasn't willing to pay it.'

A READER was impressed when he was on holiday in Florida and the local next to him in a pub told the barmaid: 'You're in great shape. You must work out a lot.'

She gave him a huge smile in return.

Back in Glasgow, our reader thought he would try the same in his local where he told the barmaid: 'Wow! You must work out a lot.'

'You should try it,' she told him.

SCOTTISH hospitality and friendliness is famous all over the world. A visitor from Ottawa was in a chip shop in Stornaway and ordered a hamburger supper. The lady wrapped it up and then said conspiratorially: 'The hamburgers aren't very good tonight, so I've given you two.'

AN Ayrshire reader wondered if the foreign chap at Glasgow's Buchanan Bus Station ever reached his destination when he approached the driver of a parked bus and politely asked if it was going to Ayr. The driver shook his head, pointed to the bus at the next stand, and told him: 'Naw, pal. Err Err Err.'

AN ex-pat in Canada knew he was back in Glasgow when he was going through the city's airport and the uniformed chap said he would have to give him 'a wee pat doon' and asked what the lumpy object was in his pocket.

He took out a bulging wallet and the security chap sighed: 'Aye...ah huvnae seen one o' those since I was married,' and waved him on his way.

A READER was sitting beside a mother on a plane who breastfed her baby during the flight. As they were coming into land, the cheery steward checking seat belts, said to the mum:

'He was hungry!'

'Not really,' replied the mum. 'It's just that my doctor said it would help alleviate the pressure in the baby's ears.'

'Goodness,' replied the steward. 'And all these years I've been sucking sweets.'

A GLASGOW couple splashed out on an upmarket hotel in Spain where they found themselves lounging at the pool beside a history professor and his wife.

The prof turned to the Glasgow chap and asked: 'Read Marx?'

'Yes,' he replied. 'I think it's those wicker chairs.'

AMONGST our favourite cruising stories was the reader on an American cruise, when the passengers went ashore in Mexico, were handed a postcard of the liner which they could show to any taxi driver to take them back to the dock if their Spanish wasn't up to it and the driver didn't speak English. So, he duly flashed the card at a taxi driver, but it didn't quite work. He drove them to the post office.

A PARTICK reader on holiday in Wales tells us he visited the local cinema where the glass-fronted message board outside said the film that evening was on at 6:59.

When he bought his ticket he commented on the time being very exact.

'We've lost our number seven,' the ticket-seller explained.

A READER who retired to France enjoys watching episodes of *Taggart*, which are shown on local TV with French subtitles. He realised how challenging that can sometimes be as two officers came out of a chip shop and handed a supper to Inspector Taggart who angrily shouted after opening the bag: 'Where's ma pickled onion?' The French translation on screen said simply: '*Bon appétit!*'

AN American visitor to Scotland says when he was visiting Stratford-upon-Avon he asked a local what St George's Day was all about.

'It's like St Patrick's Day,' the chap replied. 'But without all the fuss.'

AUSTRALIA was having a tough time of it with flooding, and one of the most heart-breaking stories was the *Morning Bulletin* newspaper in Queensland reporting that 'Thirty thousand pigs were floating down the Dawson River'.

The newspaper put an apology in the following day which read: 'What piggery owner Sid Everingham said was thirty sows and pigs.'

WE have long been admirers, as we've said before, of Australian plain speaking. A report in *The Herald* about allowing tattooing in Scottish prisons referred to previous

Australian research. A member of the Scottish Prison Service tells us:

'Our study is called "Tattooing in Scottish Prisons: A health care needs assessment". The Australian university research published in the *Australian Health Review* was entitled "Jaggers in the Pokey".'

HOLIDAYING at Easter was a Glasgow chap who had been persuaded by his family to go pony trekking in the Lake District. Being a tad dubious about the venture, he asked his wife, as they were putting on their riding helmets and surveying the four-legged beasts in front of them:

'How can I pick the slowest one?'

'Put a bet on it,' his wife replied. 'That usually works for you.'

A READER in Australia declared: 'I saw a car in Sydney with a sticker on the back window saying, "I Miss Glasgow."

So I smashed a window, nicked his radio, and left a note stating, "Hope this helps".'

'I GOT an email from a hotel company saying if I booked a holiday then my kids could go free,' said the chap in a Glasgow pub the other night.

'Things must be bad if they've turned to kidnapping,' he added.

FELIX McCoy, retired head concierge at the unforgettable

Albany Hotel in Glasgow, tells us they once had an American flight attendant who asked if there was a spiritualist church nearby. Felix sent a young concierge to make inquiries.

He returned with directions to the spiritualist centre in Somerset Place, then added with a straight face: 'Remember, ring the bell when you go there. Don't knock on the door. That just confuses them.'

A GLASGOW reader back from a beach holiday in the Caribbean tells us his sons amused themselves by trying to catch the names of girls on holiday with their boyfriends walking past on the beach.

If her name was, say, Anita, they would write 'Marry Me Anita' in big letters on the sand then watch the reaction when the couple walked back past them.

A JOURNALIST on one of the smaller radio stations in Scotland tells us of the day when a bulletin contained a particularly tricky surname of a Polish chap who was injured in a car accident locally. Staff were taking childish pleasure in whether the bumptious newsreader would stumble over it.

But when it came to the name, the newsreader smoothly announced: 'The driver's name has been withheld by police until relatives have been informed.'

AN attractive young woman arrived at Glasgow Central Station to catch the train to Manchester. Mindful that the last time she used the service it had been disrupted by line maintenance and she had to change trains twice, she asked the chap in the smart Virgin uniform: 'The Manchester train ... do I have to change?'

'No,' he told her, 'what you're wearing is fine.'

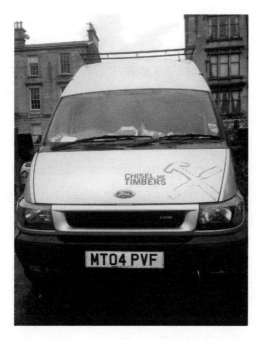

A READER flying from Leeds Bradford airport to Glasgow in a particularly rough and bumpy flight sat next to a sweating, nervous chap who tried to jump up as soon as the plane landed, but couldn't, and started shouting that he feared he'd had a heart attack.

A stewardess calmed the situation by undoing the petrified chap's seat belt, which he had forgotten about.

A READER was at the Edinburgh Military Tattoo, enthralled by the Swiss Army drummers whose complicated and fast routine received a rousing response from the crowd. As the applause died down, a chap behind him declared: 'You can certainly tell the armies with time on their hands.'

WE remember when BBC foreign correspondent Martin Patience – an Eaglesham lad – was stationed in Israel and had gone to a hotel to meet a tourist who thought he was Jesus Christ – it's a phenomenon known as Jerusalem Syndrome, as people can become mentally imbalanced surrounded by all the religious iconography there.

He was told the chap had left the hotel and, as a disappointed Martin walked away, the helpful receptionist shouted over: 'Wait. We've got a John the Baptist if that's any help.'

ROY Hay in Australia tells us of a local club where members were taking part in a charity parachute jump. As part of their training, the instructor was telling them to prepare themselves for landing once they were about ninety metres from the ground.

'How do you know you are at ninety metres?' asked one woman.

'A good question,' replied the instructor. 'At ninety metres you can recognise the faces of people on the ground.'

The woman thought about this for a while before asking: 'What happens if there's no one there you know?'

A BUSINESSWOMAN flying up from London to Glasgow last week was sitting behind a mum with her two young boys.

When the drinks trolley came round, one of the lads asked: 'Mum, can I get a Coke?'

'No,' replied the mum. 'You know why you're not allowed it.'

He argued back: 'But I'm strapped in, Mum – I can't go hyper.'

THE holiday stories continue to land on our desk as a reader tells us about him and his wife visiting elderly friends, taking with them the dreaded holiday photos.

'That's me in my sun hat and sunglasses – I was incognito that day,' chirruped his wife to the couple.

'I don't know how you remember the names of all the places you've been,' replied the elderly lady.

A READER flying back to Scotland was at an American airport where one of the ground crew at the departure gate was speaking into her walkie-talkie, or whatever they are called these days, and telling another member of staff:

'Please disregard the call for wheelchair assistance at gate A5. Repeat. No wheelchair needed at gate A5.'

There was the squawk of the person at the other end replying, before the crew member said wearily: 'Yes, it's a miracle.'

WE return to Aussie plain speaking. Retired Aussie diplomat Richard Woolcott tells in his book *Undiplomatic Activities* of former Australian Prime Minister Bob Hawke leaving his Japanese audience bewildered when he used the Australian colloquial phrase 'I am not here to play funny buggers' after he was asked what he thought was a cheeky question.

The Japanese translator told the audience Bob had replied: 'I am not here to play laughing homosexuals with you.'

A SCOTTISH teacher at an international school in Cairo tells us her class trooped in last week, and when the last pupil left the door open, she automatically asked: 'Who was born in a barn?'

Her puzzled Lebanese pupil asked: 'Was it Jesus, miss?'

A GLASGOW student spent the summer working at a wildlife park in Canada. He had to tell owners of soft-topped cars that they couldn't drive through the park in case the bears tore at the roof. 'How about if I just put the top down?' one woman asked him.

WE have made fun of Americans, and now a reader living in the United States returns the compliment by sending us a cutting from a Texan newspaper which states:

'A dying Scotsman on his death bed looked up and asked if his wife was there. "Yes, dear, I'm right next to you," she replied.

'"Are my children here?" he asked.

'"Yes, Daddy, we're all here," they said.

'"Then why the heck is the light on in the kitchen?" he asked.'

A READER in Sydney swears that a young toper in his local bar announced: 'I got attacked by a great white shark out on the surf.'

'Did you punch it on the nose?' asked an interested onlooker.

'No,' replied the swimmer, 'he just attacked me for no reason.'

GLASGOW Comedy Festival performer Vladimir McTavish tells us some expatriates in Kuwait, denied pork products, asked if he could smuggle them in some pork pies when he was going out for a gig.

'Getting six pork pies in a condom up your backside is no joke,' he adds.

WE should mention the American lady on board the *Waverley* paddle steamer on the Clyde who gushed about the scenery before adding: 'And it was made all the more memorable by the sound of the deckhands chatting away to each other in Gaelic.' No one wanted to spoil her idyll by explaining that the *Waverley* had gone the way of many Glasgow-based companies by hiring a number of Polish chaps.

A GOLF club philosopher asks us: 'Why do the folk who get kicked off of *The X Factor* always say that this isn't the last you'll see of them. As I've no intention of holidaying at Butlin's, I'm pretty sure it is.'

ALISTAIR Sloan in Ayr was at the Jim Bowen show at the Fringe where an Edinburgh girl was asked in the general knowledge part of the game show: 'Which old queen was retired to Long Beach, California?' She answered: 'Liberace.'

A CHAP in the pub the other night was telling his pals that he had been quite nervous on a recent flight when he discovered that the pilot was female.

'Oh, that's so sexist of you,' one of his mates replied. 'It's not as if she had to reverse it.'

A READER back from holiday in Guernsey relates that some fun-loving young Glasgow women were staying at the same hotel. One morning, they were discussing what they got up to the night before. One of them was being accused of getting over-amorous with a chap, but she defended herself: 'Leave us alone. Nothing happened – we were just talking, that's all.'

'Don't talk tripe, Mags,' retorted a pal. 'You had his shirt aff faster than a nurse applying CPR.'

HOLIDAY problems we had never thought about. Neil Gibson and wife flew off on holiday last week, and his good lady, not wishing to leave the car keys lying around an empty house, planked them in the oven. The only problem was, she hadn't counted on their dutiful daughter coming round to the house the day before they returned to bake a birthday cake – which came out to the aroma of melted plastic, and a car outside that could no longer be unlocked.

A READER visiting Lord Nelson's HMS *Victory* in Portsmouth tells us that the tour guides naturally take the history of the ship very seriously. And our reader tells us it just had to be a Scottish voice that shouted out on the tour, when the guide reverently pointed out the plaque on the spot where Nelson fell: 'I'm no' surprised. I nearly tripped ower it ma'sell.'

READER Jock Clark in Kilmacolm returned from a touring holiday to Italy, Slovenia and Croatia. An elderly lady on the trip was often seen carrying a large box around with her. Jock's curiosity eventually got the better of him and he asked what it contained.

'It's a cyclamen plant,' she explained. 'I didn't trust anyone at home to look after it while I was away.'

DEREK McCann in Aberdeen was flying from Atlanta to Orlando in the United States when a family of four behind him in the queue were told there were only two remaining seats. At that the grumpy mother announced she and her daughter would take them and her husband and son could get a later flight, for all she cared.

Later on board the plane Derek heard the woman ask a steward if he knew what had happened to her missing husband and son.

Says Derek: 'When the attendant told her they were in fact up in business class, her face was a picture.'

OUR mention of Arran reminds John Thomson in Hamilton of going on an open-top bus tour of the island in which the driver's running commentary, desperate for interesting things to tell them, intoned: 'This is Whiting Bay, site of the longest pier on the Clyde.'

And after a short pause: 'But it's no' there any longer.'

A MILNGAVIE reader returning from holiday in Ireland liked the insouciance of his Dublin taxi driver when he urged him to step on it as he had a plane to catch.

When the driver asked when the plane was taking off, our reader replied: 'An hour!' But his driver told him: 'Sure we'll have time for a pint on the way.'

A READER holidaying in Spain was lying at the pool beside an extended Scots family when the wife announced to hubby she was going shopping with her mother, and could she have her husband's bank card to extract some euros.

Our reader presumes there was a difficulty in remembering hubby's four-digit PIN, as his mother-in-law returned a few minutes later and unleashed a shrieking scream so rarely heard at a Spanish swimming pool: 'Paul, when did Thistle win the League Cup?'

TALKING of airports, a reader says he was travelling back from Dublin when there was a bit of a stushie in the security queue in front of him.

Eventually he heard the security chap tell a confused woman: 'No, you don't put your baby on the tray. You can take him straight through with you.'

BURNS Night reminded an East Kilbride reader of getting in a cab in New York and noticing from the driver's licence that his name was Robert Burns.

Making conversation, our reader said to him: 'That's a famous name you have.'

'It should be,' the chap replied. 'I've been driving a cab here for nearly forty years.'

AS others see us: a reader in the US sends us a cutting from his local newspaper's fun page which states: 'Wee Jock has been crying all day because his hamster died.

'"Ye didnae cry like that when yer Granny died," says his mother.

'"Aye, but I didnae pay fer her wi' ma poacket money."'

ROBERT White, from Kirkcudbright, was on a late night bus in Glasgow when two women came on, slightly unsteady, but still carrying shopping bags.

Says Robert: 'The bus stopped sharply and one of them yelled, "Ma tomatas are rollin' doon the bus." Her shopping bag had spilled.

'I picked up two tomatoes and said, "They're a wee bit bruised and dirty. You'll not be able to eat them now."

'"Och, son. That's okay. They're no fur me. They're ma man's. He'll no ken they've been rattling aboot the bus."'

SLEEPING on trains stories remind Alastair Macpherson of the Aberdeen University student who used to travel by train to his home in Keith every Friday evening. Says Alastair: 'Unfortunately, he often fell asleep and didn't wake up until the train reached the end of the line in Inverness.

'So, he wrote "Keith" on a large piece of cardboard and

hung it round his neck before dozing off as usual. Imagine his chagrin when a member of the train staff woke him up, telling him, "Hello, Keith. You'll be delighted to know that you are now safely in Inverness.'"

A RETIRED sports journalist tells us about accompanying an Old Firm team to Eastern Europe when the chatty pilot on the chartered plane announced he wouldn't be at the game himself as he and his co-pilot were taking the two stewardesses out for dinner.

On the flight back to Glasgow following a nil-all draw, the pilot came on to tell the team: 'Sorry about the result. If it's any consolation, we didn't score either.'

RECENT weather has made a few Scots think of buying a holiday home abroad. The story goes of one couple visiting Portugal who were told by the local bar owner of the lovely cottage next to his being up for sale. After they bought it, he told them that it needed some work as the roof leaked in the winter and the plumbing was shot to pieces.

'Why didn't you tell us that before?' they asked.

'Weren't neighbours then,' he replied.

IAN McLean saw an American couple in Glasgow city centre looking at a poster advertising sightseeing excursions by the company Mercat Tours.

'Arnold, do you want to come and see the meerkats?' one of them asked her partner.

A GLASGOW reader hears two women discussing a mutual friend with one of them saying their pal had been on a ballooning holiday. When the second lady expressed surprise, the first one added: 'Aye, she came back three stones heavier than when she went.'

WHEN the Berlin Wall came down we were told by a Scottish doctor that he attended a medical conference in Berlin in the 1980s where a local medic took him to see the wall.

He told us: 'Directly opposite was a tower with an East German armed guard. Between us and the wall was a fence, then a no-man's-land of bare ground. Directly under the guard, written on the wall was "Gers Ya Bass".'

'I started laughing. My German friend asked what was so amusing, and I explained.

'He was dumbfounded. "You mean that someone risked his life to write a football slogan on this wall, where so many have been shot? This has been on the wall for a year – we had no idea what it meant, or even the language it was in."'

6

Drink to That

For many people, a visit to the pub became just a memory this year. Here are some tales of happier times standing in front of the bar staff.

THE chap in the Glasgow pub was being bought drinks by mates after his wife had given birth. Recounting the event, he told them:

'When the wife was in labour the nurse came in and said: "How about epidural anaesthesia?"

'So I told her, "Naw you're alright, hen, we've already picked a name."'

THE chap in the Glasgow pub told his fellow topers: 'Did you see that it was so cold in Northern America that the town of Hell froze over?'

'I'm away home then,' announced one of his pals.

'You'll never guess what the wife promised me if that ever happened.'

A READER was in a Glasgow bar when a chap walked in, and his pals expressed astonishment he was there.

'Thought you had to stay in?' asked one.

And he replied: 'Well the phone rang and the wife said, "Pretend I'm not in." So I came straight here.'

RETIRED police officer Bobby Shaw, told us: 'I was in a pub in Greenock where I asked, "Do you have access to wi-fi?" But the barman replied, "Ah don't even have access to ma weans."'

WE thought the chap was being particularly louche in the pub the other night when he was discussing the hot weather with an attractive blonde. When she said she fancied a car with a sunroof, he told her with a straight face: 'Yes, it would give you a bit more leg room.'

THE centre of Glasgow was assailed by large numbers of ladies seeking further refreshment after a charity lunch at the Hilton. One chap in a smart bar was approached by one such lady who told him:

'You look like my third husband.'

'Bloody hell,' he said. 'How many husbands have you had?'

'Two,' she replied.

SAYS Rod Macdonald: 'When I first came to Glasgow I was having a drink in the Park Bar with two friends. One of them insisted that we go to the marvellous Pot Still where they had hundreds of different bottles of whisky. He eventually persuaded us to get a taxi there, and I had a pint of lager, my other mate had a vodka and he had a Bacardi and Coke.'

BAR story from Perthshire where a reader tells us: 'A local character in Auchterarder ordered a hawf and a hawf, announcing to the barman that he was sixty-two today.

'The barman said, "Have that one on me." Thanking the barman for his generosity he then proceeded to inform the bar that next week he was two to ten.'

A CHAP in a Glasgow pub was being asked by his pals how his date with a dentist had gone.

'She said she had a great time,' he told them, 'and that she would like to see me again in about six months.'

'I GOT aroused watching *Countdown* the other night,' said the loudmouth in the pub. 'Not bad – seven letters,' he added.

A TERRIBLE thing the drink. A Glasgow reader was in a city bar beside two chaps who had clearly been on the sauce most of the day. One of them nudged his pal, pointed across the bar and told him: 'Look at the state of them. That'll be us in ten years.'
  'That's a mirror, ya eedjit,' his pal replied.

A CHAP in the pub said he couldn't help it when his wife looked up from her magazine and announced:
  'It says here it would improve your sex life if you just walked twenty minutes a day.'
  He replied: 'Why? Who do I know that lives twenty minutes away?'

AH, the pub banter. A Glasgow chap arrived in his local, took out his smartphone and showed his pals a photo of his new girlfriend while observing:
  'She's beautiful, isn't she?'
  'If you think she's gorgeous, you should see my girlfriend,' replied one of the chaps.

'Why? Is she a stunner?' he replied.

'No, she's an optician,' came the droll reply.

A CHAP about to take a drink in a Glasgow pub was interrupted by the toper next to him who said: 'I wouldn't touch that Tennent's Lager if I were you – it'll make your teeth fall out.'

'Why would that happen?' asked the puzzled chap.

'Because it's mine,' the drinker replied.

A READER in a Glasgow pub heard a young chap further up the bar who was sipping a soft drink decline the offer of a pint with the remark: 'I'm allergic to alcohol.'

As this surprised the folk with him, he added the explanation: 'Whenever I take it I break out in handcuffs.'

WE pass on the tale from actor Iain Robertson who explained on social media: 'I heard a story last night about a pal of mine who used to be a bevy merchant. He got steaming in Glasgow, blacked out and woke up in Vienna, but thought he was in Dundee. When ma pal said, "How did ye think it was Dundee?" He says, "The buses wur the same colour."'

A GLASGOW reader swears to us that he heard a young chap in his local announce: 'My girlfriend's threatening to leave me because she claims I'm more interested in playing poker than in her. I think she's bluffing.'

'WHAT'S your favourite beer?' a market researcher asked a chap in Sauchiehall Street last week. 'Oh, probably the fifth one,' he replied.

A DRINKS industry sales executive recalled a rep from Tennent's going into a bar in Glasgow's down-to-earth Gallowgate and being told by the owner that he feared he might lose his licence.

When the rep asked why, the owner told him there had been a fight on the premises on Friday night.

As this was a regular occurrence, the rep reassured him that he shouldn't lose his livelihood over it.

'The police were in,' the owner continued, but again the rep tried to reassure him it was a common enough occurrence for police to be needed.

'No' wi' horses they're no',' replied the glum owner.

OUR old *Herald* chum Jack McLean was most put out when he went into a Shawlands bar where he was asked to remove his trademark fedora. It seems that bars with CCTV want customers to be bare-headed so that they can be identified if they cause trouble.

It is aimed, it has to be said, to hoodie or baseball cap-wearing troublemakers rather than elegant chaps in fedoras.

Jack's telling remark to the barmaid, 'So I suppose you wouldn't serve Humphrey Bogart in here?' lost much of its impact when she asked who Humphrey was.

WE suppose he couldn't resist it, the chap in the West Lothian bar who asked for an orange juice. The barmaid turned away, hesitated, then turned back and asked: 'Still orange?'

And he replied: 'Yes, I've not changed my mind.'

ALLAN Kelly in Perth recalls a charge-hand, from when Allan worked as a student barman, who bought large bottles of mixers from the wholesalers, and after-hours would refill the mixer baby bottles already used and refit the bottle tops from the bin, straightening them where necessary.

Added Allan: 'The next day he would then charge full price and pocket the takings. Of course, the flaw in his strategy was that the mixers went flat overnight as the bottles were not sealed properly, but he fixed this by looking away and making a "psshht" sound as he opened them.'

CHARLIE Andrews in Greenock heard a chap in the pub tell his pals that going home drunk the previous night had been one of his worst nights ever. When they asked why, he told them:

'I stood at the bottom of the stairs, drunk. So I decided to take off my clothes and shoes and tiptoe upstairs.' That didn't sound so bad, said his pals, until he added: 'Then I realised I was still on the bus.'

READER Tom Burnett tells us of being at a function where the speaker thanked the bar staff, Nick and Roger.

As the guests added their thanks, the speaker added: 'That's not their real names – it's just what they do all day.'

WOMEN falling out – never a pretty sight. We fear a drink or two had been taken in the West End bar at the weekend when one woman out with pals took exception to something said by one of them and replied: 'I was going to give you a nasty look but I see you already have one.'

JIM Hair in Dalry was at a pub quiz where a contestant was asked to name a fish beginning with C. 'Chuna,' the chap replied.

TALKING of the West End, a reader heard a woman entering a well-known bar there say to her pal: 'Every time I walk in here I remember my mother's wise words.

'She always told me, "Don't pick that up, you don't know where it's been."'

A READER overhears a group of lads in a large Glasgow pub working out what they are going to drink. 'It's three pounds a pint, or a pitcher for a tenner,' said one.

'Why would I want my photo taken drinking lager?' asked his pal.

THE redoubtable entertainer Andy Cameron tells us, and who are we to doubt him: 'A blonde brassy barmaid in Maryhill was stunned at the good looks of a tall handsome stranger who walked in. As she served him his pint she says, "Hivnae seen you in here afore – jist moved intae the area like?"

'"No," says the tall fella, "I live round the corner, but I've been away for twenty years and I've just come back."

'"Oh,' she giggles. "A merchant seaman are you?"

'"No, I've been in prison for murdering my wife and her mother."

'The stunned silence round the bar was only broken by the barmaid asking, "Oh, on yer own then?"'

SCOTT Barclay in Hamilton tells us about friends John and Claire visiting from Colorado who popped into Glasgow's esteemed Horseshoe Bar, where Claire asked for a gin and Slimline tonic.

The barman looked at his shelves before telling her: 'We only have full-fat, hen. Away and run round the block, and I'll watch your drink.'

'MY mate does a brilliant bird impression,' said the chap in the pub the other night. 'He takes three hours to get ready for a night out.'

A TOPER in a Glasgow bar the other night, on being asked about his weekend, replied that he had suffered 'classic withdrawal symptoms'.

Asked for further enlightenment, he replied: 'My head was sore, my bank account had been emptied out and I had three ATM receipts in my pocket.'

YOU have to be wary of what appears to be bargains offered on the internet. Said one chap in a Glasgow pub: 'I paid £200 to a firm which guaranteed to make me rich.

'Turned out they changed my name to Richard by deed poll.'

JOHN MacDonald in Dubai returned to Scotland a couple of years after decimilisation, and was shocked, after puffing on duty free, to see the price of a packet of fags in the pub's cigarette machine was a new-fangled fifty pence piece. Says John:

'I protested indignantly to the barman that I'd been ripped off – ten bob for a packet of fags. Half-a-crown was the going rate, maybe four shillings allowing for the time I'd been away, moan moan.

'The barman listened patiently to my rant, raised an eyebrow, and asked, "Ten bob, half-a-crown, shillings – hiv ye jist got oot o' jile, son?"'

BRUCE Henderson in Maybole was visiting a Glasgow pub when a chap there announced: 'Ah'm goin to ma daughter's fur ma dinner, ah always go there on a Monday.'

This communication was absorbed by his pals until one of them announced: 'But don't you know this is Tuesday?!'

'Ach, she disnae mind if ah'm a wee bit late,' the chap replied.

A GLASGOW reader swears to us he was in a bar in Finnieston when the peace and quiet was shattered by a gaggle of women arriving and demanding drink after attending a Michael Buble concert in the nearby Hydro arena. They all wanted served at once so the under-pressure barman shouted out: 'Right, let's do this the easy way. Oldest first.'

Suddenly, says our reader, you could have heard a pin drop.

ANDY Cameron tells us that the late great Glasgow singer and entertainer Glen Daly was once served a whisky with ice in it, and when he complained that he didn't ask for ice, the Glasgow barman replied: 'It's only ice – it'll no' dae ye any harm.'

'Tell that tae the captain o' the *Titanic*,' replied Glen.

A READER in Sussex tells us the Scottish reputation for meanness is even exploited by native Scots. He was in his local where there was a dispute between drinker and barman on whether he had proffered a £10 or a £20 note for his drink.

Our reader then heard the toper tell the barman: 'I'm Scottish, so I know exactly how much money I had.'

Faced with this irrefutable logic, the barman immediately gave him the change from a twenty.

THERE used to be a pub on Glasgow's challenging Paisley Road called the Burns Cottage, which had bands playing most evenings. A reader once recalled: 'After a band played there one night they were all invited to someone's party in Govan afterwards. There was a sing-song and when the band's singer was asked to give them a number he loftily declared that he only sang for money. A penny was thrown at him with the instruction, 'Now sing.' He did.

A READER heard a young chap in his local pub tell his pals: 'I pulled up the duvet cover on my bed and my hand slipped and I accidentally punched myself in the face. Not to worry though – I've had it coming for some time.'

ONE of Glasgow's best whisky bars is the Pot Still. We did like its chutzpah when someone complained on the travel site TripAdvisor that they were ignored when they arrived at the bar.

Pot Still management viewed the security tape and replied on TripAdvisor: 'You came to the bar at 13:32:51, you turned away at 13:33:11 so all told you spent twenty seconds waiting before leaving.

'The youngest Scotch we sell waits three years in cask before it's even considered a whisky, let alone ready to be bottled. The oldest whisky we have waited fifty years before being bottled. When it went into cask, no one knew who Sergeant Pepper was and the UK was trying to get INTO Europe.

'If you feel twenty seconds is too long in your life to hang on in that company, then maybe you're not ready for whisky yet.'

7
That's a Date

The emotional minefield of dating has always led Scots into humour.

SOME young lads in the pub were discussing how suspicious their girlfriends were. One lad topped the stories by declaring: 'I took the girlfriend for a romantic weekend in Paris and when we got there I pointed over and said, "There's the Eiffel Tower." She just threw me a dirty look and snapped, "I thought you said you'd never been to Paris before?"'

A GLASGOW chap was being asked how he was getting on with the girl he had recently met. 'She texted me, "Your lovely,"' he explained to his pals, 'and I texted back, "'No, YOU'RE lovely." Now I can't get rid of her, even though all I was doing was correcting her grammar.'

A READER from Bearsden emails: 'I was telling my son how technology was making his life a lot easier than mine when I was his age, and when he asked for an example I told him that he will never experience the anxiety of calling a girl's phone number and having to ask her dad if she's home.'

A GLASGOW reader swears he heard a young woman criticising her pal for drinking too much and the pal defending herself by saying: 'What's wrong with fancying a man in a uniform?' But her pal replied: 'Honey, he was a statue of a pilot in a travel agent's doorway.'

'A BLOKE in the pub last night,' says a reader, 'asked his girlfriend if he was the only one she had ever been with. He said she confirmed that he was, then added: "All the others were nines and tens."'

THOUGHT-PROVOKING comment from a Hyndland reader who emails: 'Nobody says, "What are you going on about?" more than a man who knows exactly what you are going on about.'

A CRUSHED young reader admits: 'I was the only one in a lift when an attractive girl came in, talking on her phone. She told her friend, "I have to go, there's a cute guy here." Before I could even react, she turned to me and said, "Sorry for lying, I really wanted to get off the phone with her."'

A GLASGOW reader heard a chap in a city centre wine bar ask a woman with her pals if he could take her out. She gave him a long look before replying: 'Out of what? My comfort zone?'

EVER take revenge on a former boyfriend or girlfriend? A reader in Dublin says a girl on a bus was telling her friend that every week she still plays the same Lotto numbers as her ex. She explained that if he ever won he would have to cope with the news that the millions were divided in half and he had to share it with his former girlfriend.

THERE was the chap who made dinner for his new girl-friend and told her:

'Those chips you've just eaten actually came from my garden this morning.'

'Wow,' she smiled, 'I didn't know you grew potatoes.'

'I don't,' he told her. 'Some drunk must have thrown them over the hedge last night.'

A YOUNG Glasgow lad in his local bar was telling his pals: 'I got a text from the girlfriend saying "Love you babe xxx" and after I replied "Love you too", she said it would mean a lot to her if I started putting 'x's at the end of my texts.

'So, I ended my next text with "Olivia, Heather, Sophie and Kirsty" and somehow all hell broke loose.'

ONE of the Scottish soldiers on a tour of duty in Afghanistan was getting such a slagging for putting up a picture of his much cared-for Peugeot hatchback with alloy wheels while all the rest of the squadron sported pictures of their girlfriends.

The car chap eventually snapped back: 'Laugh if you want – at least my car will still be there when I get back.' As he came from Glasgow's notorious Milton housing scheme, his squadron mates told him that was a pretty big boast.

A WOMAN in Glasgow's West End was telling her pal about the benefits of going to see a therapist. 'It's great,' she said. 'You spend an hour just talking about yourself. I suppose it must be like being a bloke going out on a date.'

'I THINK my girlfriend had sixty-one boyfriends before me,' said the loudmouth in the bar the other day. 'At least,

I think that's what she means when she calls me her sixty-second lover.'

A READER met a woman called Norah Knight and thinks he may have worked out why she never had a boyfriend from Glasgow.

WHEN the office Christmas parties began a reader overheard a gently swaying chap approach a colleague in a Glasgow bar and ask her out.

'No, sorry, I would be cheating,' she replied.

'What? Have you got a boyfriend?' the chap persisted, before she delivered the killer line.

'No. I would be cheating myself.'

'A SAW this cute young thing in the bar on Saturday night,' said the pub loudmouth. 'So, I went up and asked her what her name was.

'"Chantelle," she said.

'So I told her, "Come on, you can tell me."'

THE course of true love doesn't always run smoothly, as a reader tells us of being on a train going into Glasgow when a young chap sitting opposite told his pal:

'She said she would think about going out with me if I got a job. So I told her, "What makes you think I would want to go out with you if I had a job?"'

'I ASKED my girlfriend what she wanted for her birthday,' said the chap in the pub the other night. 'So with a big smile she held up her left hand and wiggled her third finger.'

He then added: 'Gloves it is then.'

'THE girlfriend,' said the chap in the pub, 'was constantly nagging me about getting married, so to shut her up I said we could have a summer wedding.'

'July?' asked his mate.

'Of course I did,' the chap replied.

'DO you ever miss the ex?' a woman meeting her girlfriends for a drink asked in Glasgow's West End.

'Oh all the time,' replied one of her pals. 'You wouldn't believe how much.'

'But I thought you hated his guts?' replied the first woman.

'Wait, did you say ex or sex?'

A WOMAN having coffee with friends in Glasgow was discussing her new boyfriend, and mentioned she had reservations about him having such a hairy back.

'How hairy is it?' eagerly asked a pal.

'Put it this way,' she replied, 'I'm worried that if we go on holiday this summer, animal rights activists will throw red paint over him.'

A GLASGOW reader tells us she held her breath when her young daughter peered keenly into the face of her unmarried aunt and asked: 'Why have you so many laughter lines?'

Auntie, though, merely replied: 'It must be all the clowns I've dated.'

A READER swears to us he was in a boisterous city centre bar last weekend where he heard a woman tell her pals: 'I just wish more of my handcuff stories involved boyfriends and no' the polis.'

GLASGOW chap in the pub told his mates: 'I asked the wife what women really wanted and she said, "An attentive lover." Or it might have been "a tent of lovers" – I wasn't really listening.'

A READER out socialising in Glasgow's city centre at the weekend was impressed by the insouciance of the chap in the bar who was asked by the young woman he was talking to:

'What would you do if you had a million pounds in the bank?'

The chap merely replied: 'Wonder where the rest of it had got to.'

OUR tales of romantic Glaswegians remind a reader of hearing a young chap in a city pub tell his pals: 'Yes, I love her – I'd take a bullet for her. Well, in the leg, anyway.'

NOT everyone meets a future partner in the pub. A Newton Mearns reader was at her local gym where two other women were watching a well-muscled chap work out furiously. They were debating whether he was single, with one of them coming up with the argument: 'Of course he is. Nobody works out as hard as that when they're in a healthy relationship.'

A STIRLING reader tells us the best man recently ended his speech by announcing: 'As you might know, me and my wonderful girlfriend have been together for five years. I've had a few drinks but I hope you'll indulge me if I ask her a very special question.' He then rummaged in his pocket and, as tension in the room rose, he finally fished out his car keys and said: 'I'm a bit drunk, love. Could you drive home?'

A READER hears a woman in the West End tell her pals: 'I just want a man who'll drag me to the bedroom, throw me on the bed – and do the dishes while I take a nap. Is that too much to ask for?'

NOT everyone likes smokers, it has to be said. A Lanarkshire reader at a New Year party tells us that a young chap there kissed a girl at midnight who told him, with a certain look of disgust: 'Yuck. You smoke? It's like kissing an ashtray.'

The chap tried to preserve his dignity by telling her: 'That's some strange hobby you've got.'

A GLASGOW reader getting the train into town swears he heard a woman bumping into an old pal tell her: 'I recently ended a three-year relationship.' She then added: 'It's okay, though, it wasn't mine.'

AH, going out on the pull. Irish journalist Aoife-Grace Moore remarked this week: 'God grant me the confidence of the man on a stag do in Sligo, who tried to chat me up, and once I told him I was engaged, moved onto my mammy beside me and opened with, "Is her father in the picture?"'

AS St Valentine's Day approached, a reader tells us: 'My girlfriend asked if I had something special planned for Valentine's Day. I said I was working on it, and she gave me a big smile. Which is odd, as I thought she'd be upset that I'm having to work on Valentine's Day.'

SITTING in the sun outside a West End bar, we hear a female tell her pal that perhaps her friend's new boyfriend was a tad on the diminutive side. However, her friend was taking no criticism.

'He may be four foot six,' she replied, 'but if he stood on his wallet he'd be six foot four.'

WE overhear a chap in the bar tell his mates: 'I'm always falling out with the girlfriend. I told her that in the six months we'd been together we hadn't agreed on one thing. "Seven months," she replied.'

'FELL out with the girlfriend,' said the chap enjoying a Fair Friday pint with his mates.

'She said she wanted to discuss our future. I said it would

be exciting, with personal rocket ships to transport us around the world, and bionic limbs if we ever lost one.

'But apparently that's not what she was talking about.'

'A REAL woman is a man's best friend,' declared the chap in the pub. 'She'll reassure him when he feels insecure, comfort him after a bad day, and inspire him to do things he never thought he could do. She'll help him express his emotions, give in to his most intimate desires, and always make him feel like the most confident, sexy man in the room.

'No, wait – I'm getting mixed up with alcohol.'

'NEVER date a woman whose father calls her Princess,' said the loudmouth in the pub the other night. 'Chances are she believes it.'

THE young woman draining the glass of cava on Friday night in Glasgow was overheard telling her friends: 'He's got a twenty-five-year mortgage on his flat, has had a season ticket to Ibrox for ten years and has a five-year loan on his car. And then he tries to tell me he's afraid of commitment.'

WE overhear a Glasgow woman arguing that a mutual friend's boyfriend was a tad on the short side. Or, as she declared: 'Small? Put it this way, when it rains, he's the last to know.'

DATING, it seems, is still a complicated business. A reader in a Byres Road pub heard a young student-type tell his pal that he had split up with his girlfriend. The chap then added: 'The day after she dumped me, she phoned to ask how you change your relationship status on Facebook.'

A READER having a quiet pint in Glasgow's Sloan's Bar before heading home after work, was shocked by, but also a little bit in awe of, the chap sitting further along the horse-shoe bar who answered his phone, out of which a female voice could be heard asking him where he was.

The chap had the nerve to reply: 'Do you remember when we were walking through the Argyll Arcade and we stopped to admire a diamond eternity ring in the jeweller's window, but we thought it was too expensive?' Then he added after a pause: 'Well, I'm in the pub opposite it.'

'WHEN I met my girlfriend,' said the chap in the Glasgow pub the other day, 'she said she loved a man with a sense of humour.'

He added: 'Now all I get from her is the complaint, "So is everything just a joke to you?"'

'I DON'T think my girlfriend is the brightest,' said the chap in the pub. 'When I told her that they sometimes perform cavity searches at airports looking for drugs, she said surely you couldn't hide much drugs in your mouth.'

A READER realised how rocky the path of true love is in Glasgow when he heard a young girl on Byres Road snap at her boyfriend: 'You're always slagging me off.'

'No I'm not,' he replied. 'When did I do that?'

'In the pub,' she told him.

'You're supposed to slag folk off in the pub,' he told her exasperatedly.

'DID you hear that Duncan's gettin' married?' asked the loudmouth in a Glasgow pub at the weekend. 'Ah telt him how happy ma marriage had made me,' he continued. 'But he's still goin' through wi' it anyway.'

WE recall the morose chap in the pub who told his mates that he had mixed up his Valentine cards. As he told them: 'Now my girlfriend thinks I love her, and my wife thinks I want to sleep with her.'

TRYING to think of something interesting to tell his mates, the chap in the pub announced: 'My new girlfriend once went out with a professional clown.'

'I guess you've got some pretty big shoes to fill,' a pal replied.

INTERNET dating continued. A Glasgow woman was telling her pals that the latest chap she met for a meal was perhaps not too sophisticated.

When she told him before ordering that she liked her meat rare, he replied: 'What? Like lions or tigers?'

NOSTALGIA alert! We asked for your dating stories, and Ian McCloy tells us of growing up in Port Glasgow where, as a nervous teenager on his first date, he sheltered down the back close of his date's tenement building.

Says Ian: 'Leading me to the brick-built dustbin store and out of the icy blast, my date ran her fingers over the lids of the galvanised dustbins and announced that she was going to sit on that one.

'"Why that one?" I asked.

'"Someone has just put out the hot ashes from their fire and it will keep my backside warm," she said.'

THE course of true love doesn't always run smoothly. A reader on a bus heard a young man say to the young lady with him, who was concentrating on her mobile:

'You're always on your phone.'

Without looking up, she replied: 'You're always on ma nerves.'

DAFT gag of the day comes from a Lenzie reader who says: 'My girlfriend says that sex is better when you are on your holidays. Well, that's a postcard I wasn't expecting.'

OUR tales of tenement life reminded David McJimpsey in Cumbernauld of the classic yarn:

'Two older women are leaning out of their tenement windows in the 1960s chatting, when two teenage girls with beehive hairstyles, miniskirts and high heels walk past.

'One woman declares, "Look at they two. That's all the young yins think aboot these days – sex. It wasn't like that in oor day. We were too busy hivin weans."'

8

Class Act

Out of the mouths of babes is often the start of a funny story as we hear about what our youngsters get up to.

WE hear from an East End Glasgow primary school where a firefighter in uniform was invited along from the local station to give a safety talk to pupils about the dangers of fire.

Summing up what he had told the kids about safety around the home, he asked the class:

'And why do you not touch a cooker or toaster?'

First pupil with his hand up replied: 'Fingerprints.'

A NURSE delivering a sex-education lesson to a class of first-year pupils in Glasgow held up a condom and asked what it was. Everyone in the class knew.

She then took out a courgette to show how to apply said condom and someone asked: 'What's that?'

A READER was chatting to a friend in Edinburgh who is a music teacher. She'd decided to jazz up the certificates she presented to pupils by using sealing wax to make them look more imposing, but wondered if shops still sold it.

She realised how difficult a task it was after phoning a number of stores to no avail, until one assistant asked her: 'I've never heard of anyone polishing their ceilings. Would floor wax not do?'

BOB Byiers recalled when his children were at primary school and a classmate wrote in her news book about her mummy's tights falling into the soup from the clothes-drying pulley above the kitchen table. 'The poor wee girl,' says Bob, 'had not yet learned that there was a silent "gh" in tights.'

A GLASGOW teacher tells us while discussing the human body she asked her class if anyone had ever broken a bone. One wee lad put his hand up and she asked him if it had hurt. He replied: 'No.' Thinking he was just trying to be brave in front of his classmates, she then asked which bone.

'Ma sister's arm,' he replied.

CHRIS Burt from Falkirk tells us about a group of mums waiting at the primary school gate when one of the little ones came out in a blazer which was clearly too big for him.

The perplexed lad then shouted out: 'Haw, Maw! Someone's nicked ma Polos – and left me ten pence and a hankie.'

A RETIRED modern studies teacher recalled teaching a fourth-year class about the Cold War, and spotting one of the less diligent pupils staring out of the window. Attracting the boy's attention, he asked:

'I was talking about propaganda, so can you tell me what the word means?'

He stared at the teacher before blurting out: 'It's ma maw's real faither.'

A TEACHER on playground duty at a Glasgow Secondary heard a teenage girl shout angrily to a classmate:

'Did you tell Frances ah couldnae be trusted?'

She thought the reply was sheer genius. 'Naw, it wisnae me. I don't know how she found out.'

WE hear about a schoolgirl in Glasgow's West End who didn't believe her mother when she told her the school was having a dress-down day on Friday and that she didn't need to wear her uniform.

She came home in a huff as she had been the only person in uniform that day, then blamed her mother.

'How's it my fault?' asked her bemused mum.

'You didn't argue with me long enough,' replied the girl.

HALF of primary pupils cannot swim, leading to calls for more lessons at school. It reminds us of the Edinburgh PE teacher who took a class to the baths, where she sent one girl, whose costume was covered in proficiency badges, to the deep end.

She immediately got into difficulties and he had to dive in to save her. Once out the pool he asked about her awards and she told him: 'Oh, them. The cossie's my sister's.'

WISE words heard by a reader in a Clarkston coffee shop where a woman was telling her pal that she was worried that her young son seemed a bit on the short side for his age.

'Buy him an expensive new blazer,' her pal recommended, presumably from experience, 'and watch him shoot up.'

JOE Marshall in Edinburgh recalls marking prelim exams where there was a question on limestone caverns. One pupil put forward the interesting theory that 'starling tights' hung from the roof of such caverns.

SCOT John Lunn, who won an Emmy in America for his *Downton Abbey* music, once explained that he wanted to play the cello at school in Stirlingshire but they were all taken — and he was given a double bass instead.

Added John: 'So few people played the instrument, and very quickly I was dragooned into playing for every orchestra in the county even though I could barely play it, so I was forced to learn very quickly.'

And from that decision, his musical career took off.

WE bump into a trainee teacher who tells us she had an examiner checking how she was getting on. She swears to us that the examiner was impressed at all the children putting their hands up to answer a question at the end of the lesson.

The trick, she says, in order to impress the examiner, was telling the kids beforehand to put their right hand up if they knew the answer, and their left hand up if they didn't. The class looked as though they had learned from the teacher, who knew only to ask a child with their right hand up for the answer.

RECALLING his schooldays, a reader told us: 'Our school football team was dire. It reached its lowest point when during a training session the team came across a hibernating hedgehog and began to play football with it. By the time the SSPCA arrived, the hedgehog was winning 3–0.'

A TEACHER tells us that he got a phone call from an angry mother who said that her son had arrived home from gym the previous day without his towel. She expressed her distaste that someone else may have taken it, and that 'no one respects other people's property these days'.

He asked her to describe it and she said it was a striped towel with 'Disneyland Hotel' written on it.

WHEN the schools went back after the summer, an Oban reader told us: 'My wife was a primary teacher in the days when salaries arrived as cheques in envelopes which were delivered round the classrooms. One day a boy asked what was in the envelope and my wife replied, "That's my pay."

'The boy asked, "Where do you work?"'

GRANT Young tells us: 'When I attended Ayr Academy, the toilets were a haunt of smokers and offered a fair chance of escape from PE Principal Jock McLure's occasional raids, as when he charged in one end, the smokers would disappear out the opposite end.

'One day, I was, as a committed non-smoker, standing doing what the toilets were designed for doing, when the smokers scarpered and Jock stormed in. I was ordered to his office where I duly received six of the best from his Lochgelly. He said that as the only person there I must have warned the smokers.'

SOMEHOW we stumbled into tales of primary school toilets, and Ian Forrest reminds us:

'When my stepfather was teaching a new Primary 1 intake at Edzell Primary, one wee lad fae up the glens was excused to go to the toilet. Several minutes later he reappeared and asked in a loud voice,

'"Wha aboot here wipes erses?"'

'Poor fastidious John, a bachelor until fifty, had to do the honours.'

WE do like the combination of innocence and deviousness that children sometimes portray. Reader Karen Beckett in Fairly was recalling a neighbour's five-year-old who was visiting her who suddenly asked: 'Can I have an ice pole?'

Karen told her it was polite to wait to be asked.

Seconds later the child piped up: 'Is there something you want to ask me?'

A GLASGOW teacher tells us she was talking to her primary class about colours, and she had asked them what their favourite colour was.

One wee girl said 'turquoise', which was a bit different from the others, so the teacher turned to the board and said:

'That's a very good one. How do you spell it?'

The girl immediately said: 'I meant to say red.'

A RETIRED teacher memorably tells us:

'When I had a Primary 3 class they wrote a daily news page to encourage their handwriting, grammar, spelling and sentence extension. Didn't know what to do when a child wrote, "I had to get up early today and help my mum push her boyfriend's van to start it before my dad came back."

'Sought advice from the Infant Mistress, as they were called in the 1980s. She said, "Tear it out and say to the child that you are sorry that you spilled your coffee on it at break time." So I did.'

TOM Strang at textbook publishers TeeJay received a phone call from a boy saying he was having trouble with a question in one of their maths textbooks.

Tom tells us: 'I looked out the question in the book and told the boy it was too complicated to explain over the phone and he should ask his teacher instead.

'"Ah cannae, mister," he whispered very quietly. "A'm sittin a test."

'Needless to say he got short shrift.'

A GLASGOW schoolteacher confronted a pupil who had

decided she was a goth, complete with too much make-up as far as the teacher was concerned.

'My grandfather used to come up from the coal mine looking like that,' he told her, but was put off his stride when she replied:

'What? Did he wear mascara, too?'

ONE pugnacious pupil, we recall, paid little attention in religious education. His exasperated teacher once ordered him to stand up and tell the class the Ten Commandments. The pupil hesitated, so to encourage him the teacher said:

'In any order you like.'

He then replied: 'Eight, six, ten, one, four, nine, five, two, seven, three.'

WE are told of a new teacher in Lochmaben, Dumfriesshire, who attempted to draw a sheep on the blackboard for her class of seven-year-olds.

'Well boys and girls, this is an easy one – what to you think that is?' She was shocked that no one answered, so she cajoled one of them: 'Come on now, Angus, what is it?'

Eventually Angus replied: 'Well, miss, um, is it a cross between a Cheviot and a Blackface?'

STORIES about presents for teachers reminded Bob Mathieson: 'Years ago, when my wife was teaching in Airdrie, a pupil regularly brought in doughnuts for her favourite teacher. When the teacher complained that this was too much, the wee lassie said it was okay, because her Mammy worked in Dalziel's bakery and smuggled them out in her knickers. Needless to say, the staffroom saw a severe shortage of doughnuts for a long time.'

AND reader Willie Downs passes on: 'There was the wee lad who gave a small but lovely bunch of flowers to his teacher, saying, "I'd a got you mair, miss – but the wumman chapped the windae."'

PUPILS can reveal quite a bit about their home life, and one wee boy excitedly told the class that when they were away for their summer holidays their house had been broken into. 'That's terrible,' soothed the teacher. 'Do they know who did it?'

'My dad said it was bastards,' replied the little one.

SCHOOL food stories, and Alasdair Sinclair tells us: 'When I was a prefect at Oban High in the 1950s a boy complained that he could not eat his mince as there was a maggot in it. I took the offending plateful to the teacher in charge that day. He peered at it, called for silence and said:

'"It has been brought to my notice that someone has found a maggot in his mince. When I was in the army, we were lucky to get mince in our maggots."

'Then he sat down and continued to eat his lunch.'

A MUM in Glasgow's Garrowhill wanted the spare room turned into a nursery, so she hired a jobbing painter her dad knew. Going in to the nursery to see his work, she was aghast to find that the alphabet border at head level around the room went from A, B, C, up to F, then jumped to P, Q, R.

When she angrily asked the decorator what he had done that for, he defended himself by arguing: 'What's the matter wi' ye? The wean cannae read!'

JIM MacEwan in Nethy Bridge tells us about his wife teaching in an Aberdeen primary where stories were being written about cavemen.

One girl's essay had a small spelling error. 'They had very little comfort, just a little rough matting on the floor' – with only one 't' in matting. Or at least his wife assumed it was a spelling error.

OUR tales of former pupils meeting teachers remind Joe O'Rourke of the classmate at his school many years ago who just liked staring out of the window.

Says Joe: 'The teacher used to shout at him, "You'll never get a job looking out the window all day!"

'Well, she got that completely wrong – he was a bus driver for thirty years.'

RETIRED teacher John Hodgson tells us of a primary school colleague who, attempting to make arithmetic more relevant, asked:

'If I had ten oranges in one hand and seven oranges in the other, what would I have?'

'Big hauns, miss,' came the reply.

A GLASGOW chemistry teacher tells us he fears one of his pupils may not be too excited by the subject. He noticed on the pupil's jotter that the lad had neatly stuck on the cover below the word 'Chemistry', a label from a bottle of medicine. It reads: 'Warning. May cause nausea and extreme drowsiness.'

OUR story about bird identification in the garden reminds retired teacher Margaret Thomson in Kilmacolm:

'I took my class to the park to look for birds. A wee lad yelled out, "Hey, miss, here's a burd. It's eating a biscuit!"

'I rushed over, bird book in hand. "What kind is it?"

'Came the reply, "Don't know, miss. Ah think it's a digestive!"'

TEACHER Marion Lang tells us of a ten-year-old pupil announcing to the rest of the class that, 'Ma dug did a bungee jump on Saturday.'

Says Marion: 'His classmates were very impressed, but my scepticism cast doubt on whether dogs would really be allowed to do bungee jumps.

'The answer was, "Naw ma dug – it was Mad Doug did the bungee jump!" The gentleman in question turned out to be a local worthy who was game for anything.'

OUR stories of Scots struggling to learn French remind Paul McElhone, now in Beckenham, of being so determined to pass O-Grade French, after failing previously, that he memorised an essay, 'A Day in the Country'.

Says Paul: 'When I looked at the exam paper, my heart sank. The subject was A Day in the Life of a Lighthouse Keeper.

'All was not lost, though. I began my essay by declaring that it was his day off and he was going to leave his island and go for a walk in the country. The first few sentences were a bit flaky, but the rest was perfect.'

THE first day back at school reminds us of the old yarn about the little boy telling his teacher: 'I don't want to alarm you, but my dad says that if my marks don't improve, someone's going to get spanked.'

A MOTHERWELL reader tells us his grandson came

home with a new arithmetic jotter and announced that the teacher wanted it covered, and that leftover wallpaper would do.

The little one's dad piped up: 'She's just a nosy-parker who wants to see what the inside of our house looks like.'

GREAT apologies of our time. 'In an article in the *Cumbernauld News* and *Kilsyth Chronicle*, we stated that Caitlin Henderson and her friend Calum Robinson were "the envy of their classmates" when they arrived for their school prom at Condorrat Primary School.

'However, Mrs Alison Masterson contacted us to say that her daughter was not "envious". We are happy to set the record straight and apologise for any embarrassment it may have caused.'

WHEN Phil Cairney was a teacher in Pollok he had a registration class first thing in the morning. One girl arrived late and Phil wanted to know why.

She told him: 'I was dreaming about Celtic.'

'Why would that make you late?' asked a baffled Phil.

'The game went into extra time, sir,' came the reply.

STORIES about school exams remind Russell Vallance in Helensburgh:

'My friend's daughter was recently teaching on the effects of World War One. She asked the class: "What was something specific Germany was made to do at the end of the war?"

'One girl answered: "They had to hand back Alice and Lorraine."

'Through splutters, the teacher asked who she thought Alice and Lorraine were.

'"I guess two French girls kidnapped by the Germans before the war, miss."'

INCIDENTALLY, a history teacher tells us he was tempted to give a mark to the pupil in the exam who, when asked 'What ended in 1918?', wrote '1917'.

ON the first day of the new National Five exams in Scotland's secondary schools, an exam website listed answers given by either inspired or desperate pupils to questions given in previous tests which included:

'Name six animals that live specifically in the Arctic' – 'Two polar bears, four seals.'

'Explain the phrase "free press"' – 'When your mum irons trousers for you.'

'To change centimetres to metres you?' – 'Take out centi.'

9

Don't Lecture Me

Students are our hope for the future as the country's brightest and best head off to university and college. It's just that they can be a bit daft also.

WE heard about a Milngavie teenager who moved to a student flat in Glasgow and asked his mum how to cook a meal as he had a new girlfriend coming round for dinner.

Afterwards his mum phoned to ask how the meal went, and he told her:

'Not so great. She wanted to wash the dishes.'

'What's wrong with that?' asked his mum.

'It was before I'd served the food,' he explained.

WE are told about the Edinburgh couple asking their student son to come with them to visit his gran, but he was whining that he didn't want to go as he had nothing in common with the old lady. 'I don't know about that,' his dad told him. 'You both take drugs, and I would never let either of you drive my car.'

AN Ayr reader tells us about a group of architectural students from Glasgow who were on a field trip to York where the stayed in the local university's halls of residence.

Invited to a university dinner while there, one student was perhaps overawed when he was asked at dinner by an academic further up the table: 'Which course are you on?' His startled reply of 'the soup' will haunt him for some time.

A READER claims he went to visit his student son in Dundee and, reaching the student flats, wasn't sure if he was pressing the right buzzer, so he asked the person who answered:

'Does Davey live here?'

He was concerned about the reply of: 'Aye. Just leave him there and we'll collect him later.'

A GLASGOW reader tells us the student working in the office for the summer told him: 'My dad lectured me at the weekend and said that if you really wanted something in life you had to work for it. He then turned on the telly to check his lottery numbers.'

STUDENTS have been known to collect unusual souvenirs after a drunken night out, and one confessed:

'In my first year I collected bollards, flashing yellow road-works lights, etc. Sometimes there was even a "Road Closed" sign or two. It got to the point that I could hardly move around my room, so later that night I closed off an entire road with the signs and the flashing lights.

'The road stayed closed for four whole days, with annoyed-looking drivers having to reverse out into main-road traffic. Only on the fifth day did the council come and unblock it.'

A LECTURER tells us he was at a planning meeting on future exams where a fellow member of staff produced a new set of guidance notes for students explaining what would constitute plagiarism. When she was asked if they took long to draw up, she explained: 'No, I just copied them from another college's website.'

ONE student down at Leeds told us that before she caught the train to Glasgow her mum insisted on the phone: 'Bring your laundry with you. I don't mind doing it.'

But after getting home she heard her mother on the phone to a friend: 'Typical student. She walked in the door with a big bag of washing for me to do.'

A READER hears a student in Glasgow announce that she 'wished she had a Kindle that never ran out of power'.

He wanted to rush over to her and shout: 'That's a book! You're talking about a book!'

A READER was impressed by a group of students from Glasgow Uni, which included a German lad that everyone called 'Einstein'. Our reader later learned that it was not because the chap was especially bright – it was simply because he got drunk even after just one pint.

WE recall the reader who swore to us that he attended a graduation ceremony in Glasgow where he witnessed a sobbing grandmother hug her graduating grandson and tell him: 'Your parents would have been so proud seeing you up on that stage today.'

After giving him another squeeze, she added: 'It's a shame they couldn't be bothered to come.'

TALKING of students, we were asked the other day by one: 'Where can I get a dozen spiders, mice droppings and a pool of cat pee?'

When we asked what for, she replied: 'I'm moving next

week and my landlord says I must leave the flat in the condition in which I found it.'

WE pass on the comment from American college professor Marian Viorica who is not impressed by the ability of her students to get up in the morning. As she put it: 'I once taught an eight a.m. college class. So many grandparents died that semester. I then moved my class to three p.m. No more deaths. And that, my friends, is how I save lives.'

A READER confesses: 'In my student flat we were so lazy that no one wanted to do the washing up. It dawned on us how bad it was that we found ourselves drinking whisky out of eggcups as every other cup and tumbler needed washed.'

WE liked the quote from the Glasgow professor, in a newspaper story about exam plagiarism, in which students cut and paste material from the internet, that when he was an external university examiner, one student's essay was spotted as a cheat because it ended with the phrase: 'For more information, click here.'

A DAD tells us his teenage daughter had left school and was applying for a job to tide her over before going to college.

Under 'previous employment' he encouraged her to put 'babysitting', to show that she at least had a work ethic.

When he was checking the form for her later, he noticed that after putting in babysitter, the form asked 'reason for leaving', and his daughter had written: 'They came home.'

WE once overheard a group of students discussing the virtues of buying a high-definition television screen.

'My mum came round to the flat and turned our ordinary TV into a high definition one,' declared one of them.

When asked how she managed that, he told his pals: 'She ran a duster over it.'

PETER McMahon in Kirkintilloch is reminded by our student tales of the postie delivering a letter to a West End student flat. 'Having climbed to the tenement's top floor in search of the name on the envelope, he was confronted by the final door bearing a sheet of paper with a long list of names on it which had been scored out and added to over time as the transient student occupants had come and gone.

'Not finding the name he was searching for, and reluctant to try elsewhere, he merely took the pencil which was hanging on a string, added the name from the envelope and popped said envelope through the letterbox,' says Peter.

A FORMER student, going for his latest job interview, later told his pals in a Byres Road pub:

'My dad told me to make a really good first impression. So I wasn't sure whether to open with my Sean Connery or my Frank Spencer.'

A STUDENT tells us he was in Sauchiehall Street when an ambulance was called for a girl who had been taken unwell on a night out. A lad she had met that night volunteered to go with her to the hospital, but his mate pulled him aside and said: 'Are you sure you want to do that? You've still got a couple of hours to pull someone else.'

WE didn't realise how tough it was for students these days until Jamie Kelly in Kilmacolm told us about his aunt who volunteers in a Stirlingshire charity shop where a student came in and said he needed a smart outfit as he had got a part-time job as a barman. After finding a white shirt, black trousers, belt and tie for him, she took pity on him as he was so desperate for shoes he said he would take any size between five and twelve, so she only charged him £2.50 for the outfit.

The following week, a uni minibus arrived at the charity shop crammed with students who asked for 'the wee wummin wi the glasses'.

A STUDENT at Strathclyde Uni was telling his classmates that his dad, before the term started, told him: 'You're going to be meeting a lot of girls at the university, so I got you something at the chemist's.'

As the student 'got a bit of a riddie' as he put it, his dad stammered: 'No, I meant this deodorant.'

A NORTH KELVINSIDE reader having a pint in Byres Road heard a student tell his pal:

'I'm thinking of changing my name to Domhnall.'

'Is that Gaelic?' asked his mate. 'What does it mean?'

'It's Gaelic for "hoping this will fool the Student Loans Company",' the chap replied.

ST ANDREWS University is often accused of not having enough native students. One of the Scottish students tells us: 'I heard a posh English student tell his pal the problem with his new girlfriend was that she could only speak a few words of English. He then added, "But on the plus side, Dundee girls are such great fun."'

WHEN Cardonald College merged with Anniesland and Langside colleges to form Glasgow Clyde College it reminded us of when the late great Glasgow students' charity magazine *Ygorra* made reference to a student 'who was so stupid he would have difficulty obtaining entrance to Cardonald College'.

It was claimed the college principal complained and was given the retraction: '*Ygorra* accepts that no student is so stupid that he or she would be refused admission to Cardonald College.'

WE were recalling when actor Richard Wilson was elected as rector of Glasgow University. He told the story that he was appearing in a play in London at the time and told the producer he had to go up to Glasgow for his rectorial installation.

'Is there not a hospital here in London that can do that for you?' she asked.

BEING a bit of a philosopher was the student in Glasgow's West End who told a fellow student: 'The worst part about looking for a job is, if you're successful, you end up with a job.'

THE universities will soon be back, which reminds a reader of the story about the Glasgow student who attached five £20 notes to his test paper with a note saying, 'A pound a mark.' He got the paper back with a mark of only forty, and £60 in change.

10
A Basket Case

We remember the days when shopping was a simple pleasure which could raise a smile or two.

MEAT supplier John Sword swore to us that a Glasgow butcher shop was broken into one Friday night with almost all of the stock taken. The butcher was behind the counter the next day when a wee wummin came in and asked what the matter was. He explained about the theft, then added:

'But enough of my worries. I've still got one or two things left. Do you want some chicken?'

'Just leave it, son,' she replied. 'Ma man will get it half price in the pub later.'

COMPANIES like to engage with customers on social media, so we like the chap who contacted Tesco and asked:

'Would I be able to access your CCTV? Unfortunately I was robbed at your Cardiff store today.'

Tesco replied: 'We would not give out that information to you personally. You would have to raise it with the police.'

Which is just what he wanted as he replied: 'I phoned the police, but they said Tesco charging you £17 for Gillette blades was not robbery.'

A READER shopping in a Greenock supermarket, with only a few items, was stuck behind a woman at the checkout with a large pile of groceries.

His mood wasn't helped when the woman suddenly announced: 'Oh, I've forgotten something!' and dashed back up the aisles.

He was surprised, though, when she returned a few minutes later pushing a young child in a buggy.

IN Lanarkshire, a reader was visiting his local off-licence when a young chap picked up a bottle of Buckfast wine which accidentally dropped to the floor and smashed. The shop owner called over: 'You'll have to pay for that.'

Our reader thought the young chap's reply was inspired.

'I'm not eighteen,' he stated.

A GLASGOW reader tells us he visited his late-night corner store where he asked the salesperson what time they closed.

'We close at ten o'clock,' the woman replied. 'But we start giving dirty looks at a quarter to.'

AN Edinburgh reader tells us she was in a smart Stockbridge deli when a young chap asked:

'Do you sell whales' eggs?'

The assistant thought about this briefly before asking: 'Do you mean quails' eggs?'

There was an even longer pause before the potential customer answered: 'Maybe.'

A GIRL came out of a Glasgow store and told her pal: 'I almost wet myself when I read what someone had written on a door in there.'

'What was it?' said her pal, an expectant smile already forming on her lips.

'Toilet closed,' she replied.

A READER tells us he was in a pet shop when a youngster came in and pestered his mum to let him have a pet mouse. His mother was resisting, and told him: 'Billy would end up eating it.'

'Is that your cat?' asked the shop owner.

'No, my brother,' replied the little one.

A READER was in the Edinburgh florist shop Flower when a chap came in to order a large bouquet. The florist wrote down the message he wanted on the card, then, thinking of a final flourish to add, asked: 'Will you want kisses?'

'I'll be expecting a lot more than that!' the chap replied.

A PARTICK reader spotted in his supermarket that toilet rolls were on offer at twelve for the price of nine. In addition, there was a three for the price of two offer on the packs, so he picked up six of the large packs and headed to the checkout.

As the girl scanned the huge pile of rolls, she told him: 'I'm surprised you risked coming to the shops.'

READER Cathy Macdonald was in a Largs butcher's the other day which is famous for its range of steak pies. A wee woman in front couldn't decide on what size of steak pie she wanted. The butcher, trying to help, asked how many it was to feed.

Without hesitation, she replied: 'Two and a dug.'

A CLARKSTON reader was told by his wife to pick up a star fruit on the way home for a dinner party. Driving through Bridgeton, he spied a fruiterer's and pulled over.

He asked the wee wumman serving if she had a star fruit. She looked at him for a minute, then said, 'A star fruit? Listen, son, this is Brigton. We only got bananas here two year ago.'

READER Charlie Bell was in a Dunoon charity shop where he was admiring a miniature model of the famous Liberty Bell in Philadelphia, complete with its equally famous fissure. When he asked the lady in the shop how much it was she said: 'A pound.'

Then after looking at it further, she added: 'Sorry, son, it's got a crack in it. I'll only charge you fifty pence.'

AN artist of the needle and ink tells us he tattooed a chap's name on his arm only for the chap to phone in an agitated state when he got home to claim that the tattooist had 'pit the name oan backwards'.

'Are you perhaps looking in a mirror?' the tattooist asked.

After a slight pause the phone was put down with no further discussion.

A DELIVERY man swears to us he knocked on a door in Glasgow's Southside and told the chap who answered: 'I've got a parcel for your next-door neighbour.'

The puzzled chap replied: 'You've come to the wrong house then.'

WE like the way some folk amuse themselves by leaving unusual reviews when buying products online. A reader pointed out a review on Amazon for bottles of Barrettine methylated spirit which stated:

'From the moment you remove the cap you realise you're in for a treat. Fresh, bright, smoky, with a mineral edge and rounded, fruity nose. Bold, possessing some edge and no little bite, yet remaining smooth, balanced and satisfying. This is a drink to enjoy with friends in a park. Highly recommended.'

AUTHOR Deedee Cuddihy was in a Glasgow post office when the customer behind her picked up a leaflet on items banned from international mail and read out: 'Vodka, whisky, ammunition, cannabis, cocaine, fireworks, flares, flick knives and pepper spray. Where I come from that's got the makings of a right good party.'

ANDY Leven remembered when his father ran a butcher's shop in Dennistoun in the 1960s and had a notice on the wall which stated 'CREFDIT'.

It allowed him, of course, when a puzzled customer said there was no F in Credit, to reply: 'Exactly.'

A LAID-BACK, long-haired surfer type from San Diego, California was sitting in Glasgow's Buchanan Street selling friendship bracelets he makes with a sign beside him stating, 'Handmade bracelets by this handsome guy.'

He revealed to a reader who stopped for a chat that, while he liked Glasgow, people frequently stopped and asked: 'Is the "handsome guy" away for his lunch break?'

IAN Petrie in Newton Stewart recalled: 'Many years ago a lorry loaded with Master McGrath dog food came off the A75 and landed in a field, just along from the factory where I worked. The load was lying everywhere. We were sent down to help clear up. Naturally, many "damaged" tins were being taken for dogs at home.

'One guy was filling the boot of his car and was asked if he had a dog.

'"No," he said, "but ma mither takes in lodgers."

'We hoped he was joking.'

DO we believe the jeweller in the Argyll Arcade who claims that a distraught woman came in with a picture of her recently deceased dog, and asked if a gold statue of it could be made so that she would have a permanent reminder of her faithful companion?

He says he asked her: 'Eighteen carat?'

And she replied: 'No, chewing a bone.'

AN assistant in a tile shop tells us a potential customer phoned and asked how much it cost to have her bathroom laid.

'Depends on the area,' the assistant told her.

'Carntyne,' the woman replied. 'But why would that affect the price?'

'STORE staff are getting ruder,' opined the chap in the pub the other night. 'I was in my local record store and asked if they had anything by The Doors.

'The guy behind the counter said, "Sure. A fat security guard and a *Big Issue* seller."'

THERE are a lot of sharp women out there. A reader tells us he was in a city centre barber's when the girl cutting the chap next to him asked in time-honoured tradition:

'Are you going anywhere nice for your holidays?'

'Yes, I'm going to Guantanamo Bay,' replied the customer.

'That'll be nice,' replied the hairdresser. 'And will there be any other smart alecks there?'

GLASWEGIANS have been reminiscing about the sandwich shop chain Henry Healy's, which has shut. As a lady called Maggie recalls on the website Glasgow Guide: 'My job as a junior was to pick up the bits of bacon that had fallen on the floor, put them on a tray, rinse them under cold water to remove the sawdust and make sure they were strategically placed between the nice slices so that they wouldn't be noticed, but would make up the weight.

'My family were always warned not to buy butter or bacon first thing in the morning.

'I loved every minute in that shop.'

LEADING Ayrshire coal merchant Andrew Gray in Kilmarnock told us: 'We receive very few customer complaints, but this one takes some beating.

'The customer phoned to thank us for the prompt delivery, but said he had paid the driver for eight bags and only received five. I said that our driver was very honest and would not short-deliver, and asked if he had checked the bunker.

'He said there was no need as his dog hated the coalman, and barked every time he went past the kitchen window. The dog had only barked five times.'

ALLAN Morrison in King's Park tells us: 'I have a pal who works in a bank and one day a fiscally challenged chap came in to draw money from his account. He had written the cheque in pencil and so my mate asked the customer to "ink it over".

'He came back and said, "Yes, I really, really want the money."'

WE don't know what the demand is, but cheap-products emporium Poundland in Airdrie is selling tins of yacht varnish with a nifty picture of a ship's wheel on the front.

A reader who was pondering whether Airdrie was now the Riviera of Monklands was interrupted by a fellow customer who opined: 'The only Marina I know around here works in the chip shop.'

GUS Furrie in East Kilbride tells us that his daughter was working nightshift in a local petrol station when a chap came in looking to buy cigarettes.

Says Gus: 'He looked under eighteen so she asked him for some ID.

'He said he had none, and then in a flash of inspiration said he had a tattoo, which by law you have to be eighteen to get.

'He then showed her what was clearly a home-made tattoo, so no ciggies there then.'

SOME conversations are just plain daft. We hear of the woman in the Glasgow corner shop who asked:

'Do you sell Elastoplast?'

When the shopkeeper said 'What?' the customer repeated her need for Elastoplast and the shopkeeper said: 'Oh, I thought you said something about "the last of the Apaches".'

'That film was called *The Last of the Mohicans*,' said the customer, trying to be helpful.

Now thoroughly confused, the shopkeeper replied: 'What film?'

STRANGE customer requests. Assistant Anne Morrison in a Glasgow sports emporium, Greaves, was asked by a customer if they stocked football pumps with needle adaptors.

When she confirmed they did, he asked if he could borrow one. Not expecting a game to kick off in the store, she asked why he merely wished a temporary loan instead of a purchase, and he replied that he wished to clean out the wax in his hearing aid.

Alas on this occasion his request fell on deaf ears.

WE hear about a man being grilled by a security guard in a supermarket near Partick. Says the guard: 'I saw you wandering up and down the wines and spirits aisle and you definitely put something in your bag. Open your backpack so I can check.'

The man obliges. The guard peers inside: 'Can you explain why the inside of your pack is covered in tinfoil? We assume the tinfoil is an attempt to block the signal of the security tag on the bottles when you walk out with them.'

But the man responds with admirable sangfroid. 'Some-one,' he says indignantly, 'has stolen my roast chicken!'

NOT many Scots are great linguists, it has to be said. But a reader in a branch of Superdrug in Glasgow's city centre had remembered enough French to realise that the French girl in front of him was saying to her pal: 'Why do they need suntan lotion here?'

A READER overhears a Glasgow woman tell her pals over a coffee: 'In the evening I can hear any leftover cake, and sometimes ice cream, calling to me from the fridge. 'Broccoli is strangely silent.'

OUR lunch stories reminded a lawyer: 'Advocate Donald Findlay tells of a junior counsel assisting him in a trial at the High Court in Glasgow whom he sent to fetch something for lunch.

"'Nip up to M&S. Get a tuna and sweetcorn sandwich for me and something for yourself.'"

The youth returned and gave Donald his lunch and fifty pence change. Donald pointed out he had given him a £20 note and had expected rather more.

"'But you told me to get something for myself,'" replied the lad.

"'Well, what did you get – caviar, foie gras?'"

"'No, a shirt.'"

A READER who smokes – yes, there are still a few of them – has his own little joke when he buys a disposable lighter in a newsagent's. When the chap serving inevitably flicks the lighter to check it's working, our smoker tells him: 'It's all right – I've been smoking for thirty years so I know how a lighter works. You don't have to show me.'

A BOOK recalling the history of the Naafi, which supplies food and drink to the armed forces, relates that after the Falklands War there were still many British troops on the islands who liked buying souvenirs in the Naafi shop. A bestseller was a soft toy penguin – which was made in Britain, shipped 8,000 miles to the Falklands, and then taken back to Britain by the delighted troops.

OUR supermarket stories reminded Mungo Henning:
'While dropping my car off at a back-street garage for

some work, I bemoaned the fact that I had lost a hub cap and wondered where I could buy a single one, and not a set of four. The mechanic suggested Tesco.

'My puzzled look was met by his following words, "The car park, not the shop."'

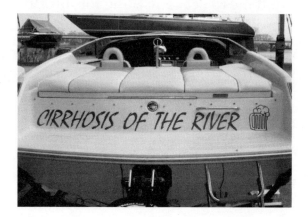

OUR stories about Christmas reminds David Martin:

'I was on a bus in Dundee and heard two girls catching up on Christmas presents.

'"My mum's got wee Joe an activity centre," one told the other.

'Obviously thinking of the Nativity scene, the other replied, "I didnae think yir mum wis religious."

'Only to be reassured, "No, no the kind o' activity centre wi' the baby Jesus, the kind wi' hammers and things."'

SCOTLAND has slipped down the international league table of pupils being good at mathematics. A Newlands reader said it reminded her of being in a shop recently buying some items which came to £12.74 and handing over a £20 note. When the assistant announced that there had been a power cut and that her till was not working so she could not work out the change, our reader told her: 'It's £7.26.'

'How do you know that?' asked the shop girl suspiciously.

WILLIAM McKinlay tells us of a business associate who was flying from Amsterdam to Glasgow for a meeting, only for the airline to lose his luggage. He was given a modest sum by the airline so that he could buy a replacement suit, but when he visited a Glasgow menswear shop and explained how much he had, the assistant told him: 'I couldn't cover you in brown paper for that money.'

11

Know the Face

Scots can be quite dismissive when they meet someone famous. Here are a few of the stories of the rich and famous encountering the Scots.

SINGER Justin Bieber popped into the Blue Lagoon chip shop for a haggis supper and a can of Irn-Bru after his show at Glasgow's Hydro where he cheerfully handed over £20 to staff.

We like an unimpressed Colin Bell on social media who commented: 'Justin Bieber comes to Glasgow and pays £20 for a haggis supper and a can of Irn-Bru? They saw you coming, mate. Absolutely stitched up.'

FILM star Al Pacino was in Glasgow taking questions from an audience about his career. After one woman shouted out a question at him in a very local accent, a puzzled Al replied:

'Like many women in my life, I love you, but I don't understand you.'

AMERICAN singer Norah Jones had one of her band whistling on one of her songs when she appeared at Glasgow's Armadillo. She told the audience that she herself couldn't whistle. She explained:

'I can't whistle blowing out the way, but I can do it a little bit drawing breath in the way. It's weird.'

To which a Glasgow voice shouted out: 'It's called asthma, hen.'

A COLLEAGUE interviewed the singer Engelbert Humperdinck in Glasgow some years ago, and took him to a bar where Engelbert began handing out autographed photos to other customers. The photo, it must be admitted, had been taken some years earlier, judging by the youthful mien.

One regular accepted the signed picture with a 'Thanks very much, Mr Engelbert', looked at it then added: 'That yer boy, is it?'

WHEN entertainer Billy Connolly was first invited as a guest to Celtic, he was about to be introduced to then owner Fergus McCann when someone whispered to Billy that Fergus was a bit of a stickler about attire and Billy should really have been wearing a tie.

Billy strode forward, shook Fergus's hand and told him:

'What kind of club is this you're running? I've only been here twenty minutes and already someone's nicked my tie!'

COMEDIAN Fred MacAulay was recalling when he walked the Great Wall of China to raise money for charity, and while there remembered that Scotland were playing in an important football tie. Working out it was now midnight back home, he thought the best option to get the result was to phone BBC security, which he did, explaining he was at the Great Wall of China and asking for the Scotland score.

He then heard the security guy say to his mate: 'I've got Fred MacAulay on, pissed in some Chinese restaurant.'

GLASGOW writer Ian Pattison was recalling the Glasgow premiere of Andrew Lloyd Webber's *Cats* at the Kings Theatre when Cameron Mackintosh, the producer, was in attendance. One of the guests was Jack Milroy, the sunnier half of Francie and Josie.

At the interval Mackintosh stopped Milroy and asked, 'How are you enjoying *Cats*?'

Jack replied, 'It's no' bad, son. But it could do with a wee dug running aboot to liven it up a bit.'

THE late Gerard Kelly, when appearing in the panto *Aladdin* at the King's in Glasgow asked the audience if he should trust the baddie, and of course the whole theatre shouted back: 'No!'

Later when Aladdin was locked in the cave, the silence was broken by a lone Glasgow voice shouting: 'Well, we telt ye.'

THE yarn was told of American actor David Hasselhoff going into a Glasgow bar while he was in the city judging the auditions for *Britain's Got Talent* a few years ago.

When the barman asked: 'What can I get you, Mr Hasselhoff?' the American entertainer cheerily replied: 'You can just call me The Hoff.'

'Okay,' said the barman. 'Nae hassel.'

ALEX Findlay in Kilmarnock swears to us that a friend of his aunt's was in a hotel where the members of the band Status Quo were in the lobby. The aunt's friend couldn't stop herself from going up to singer Francis Rossi and saying she thought she knew him, but didn't know where from.

Trying to be helpful he told her: 'Rossi.'

But she replied: 'No, son, it can't be that. I've no' been to Rothesay for years.'

GOOD to see Scottish women being explained to Americans. Paisley-born film star Gerard Butler was on a late-night chat show the other night in the States when he explained: 'You can't get away with much in Scotland.'

He said he was in a bar back in Scotland when a woman who had been staring over at him came over and said: 'You know, I know your face from the telly – but I'm not gonna tell you that, because it's going to give you a big f***ing head!'

Host Seth Meyers asked: 'Is that Scottish flirting?'

SOLDIER Blue singer Buffy Sainte-Marie, a Cree Native American, Ramblin' Jack Elliott, billed as 'America's Roving Cowboy', and Blind Gary Davis, the Black Blues great, flew into Glasgow for a folk festival some years ago.

Scottish folk luminaries Josh Macrae and Hamish Imlach were sent to collect them and, having a swift drink or two beforehand, Hamish pointed out he had only seen their faces on old album covers and asked Josh: 'How will we recognise them?'

Josh replied: 'A blind man, a Cree Native American and a cowboy? If we don't recognise them, Hamish, I'm giving up the drink.'

A LENZIE reader watching a street performer in Glasgow's Buchanan Street heard him ask a volunteer: 'Is this your girlfriend?' while looking at the young woman with him.

When the poor chap replied yes, the performer told him: 'Fantastic! So much prettier than the one you were with yesterday.'

PROFESSOR David Purdie, a guest speaker at a Trades House dinner in Glasgow, was actually on duty the night comedian Chic Murray was brought to the Western Infirmary for a check-up after he was found slumped halfway out of his car parked outside his house.

David's junior doctor, after checking him over, reported that Chic was suffering from an overdose. A surprised David asked him what Chic had overdosed on.

'Hospitality,' replied the junior.

A SCOTS businessman tells us he and three other Scots were at the exclusive K Club golf club in County Kildare, Ireland, where they were a bit boisterous while sharing the bar afterwards with movie star Clint Eastwood.

Eventually one of the Scots went over and, using Clint's classic *Dirty Harry* line, asked: 'Clint, could you make my day?'

Clint replied: 'No. But you could sure make my day by shutting up.'

Only then did he relent and agree to a picture.

SINGER Rod Stewart stopped off at one of his favourite pubs, the Wee Barrel, in Paisley, en route to Glasgow Airport where he bought all the locals a drink. An old punter in the corner failed to recognise the blond troubadour but called over: 'Thanks, son. Did you have a wee win on the horses?'

THE great investigative reporter Chapman Pincher, who died at the age of one hundred years old, wrote in his biography about his love of fishing in Scotland and revealed: 'Scottish ghillies are a breed unto themselves. I have a vivid memory of my ghillie shouting across the Dee to ask another why the owner of the beat and his guest were not fishing that day.

'The old man's yell, "They're away to Edinburgh on a drinking and whoooooring expedition," reverberated over the water.'

AN excitable tabloid newspaper told of 'The Ugly Truth' when Kate Moss, the model, caused a disturbance on an easyJet flight. It stated that: 'She was swigging duty-free vodka from her cabin baggage on board' and that 'There was also a "sweary" altercation with a fellow passenger at some point during the journey.'

A bemused reader tells us: 'Just sounds like your average easyJet flight out of Glasgow.'

READER Jim Morrison tells us: 'On a cruise a few years ago we had on board the actress Shirley Anne Field, who gave a talk on her life, and then asked if anyone had any questions. After a pause a large Scouse chap put his hand up, "Have you ever had a facelift?"

'"No," replied Shirley. "But I can give you the address of a place that does them if you want."'

AMERICAN comic and actor Steve Martin has been a frequent visitor to Scotland and once recalled: 'The first time I came to Scotland I was twenty-one. When I got off the train the streets were full of people laughing, drinking and puking. I thought this place was incredible ... and it's only Thursday.

'I assumed this was something that went on all the time. Then I learned these people were there for a rugby game between Scotland and Wales.'

SCOTS stand-up Craig Ferguson, former *Late Show* host on American television, once told of a Glasgow gig where, when he got outside, someone shouted: 'You were rubbish!' Craig went over to the guy who then told him that he had in fact been pretty good. When Craig asked him why he had shouted out he was rubbish, the chap replied: 'Just to keep your feet on the ground.'

WE mentioned Prince Philip's retiral, and Sue Forsyth in Bearsden recalled: 'When we lived in Windsor in the 1960s my father was a part-time fireman. The brigade was called to a fire at Home Farm on the Windsor Castle Estate.

'To prevent it spreading the firemen climbed up and down a ladder removing bales of hay two at a time. Prince Philip came to help. He was then challenged as to why he was only carrying one hay bale instead of two. His reply was, "Because you lot are being paid to do this and I am doing it for fun!"'

ACTOR and comedian Kate Robbins once told of being introduced to Princess Anne at a charity show.

During the pre-show line-up, Anne chatted briefly with Kate and asked the question that royals have asked ordinary people for decades: 'And what is it that you do for a living?'

'I'm an impressionist,' said Kate.

'Do you have an exhibition on anywhere?' Anne asked.

YOU'VE got to love Hue and Cry singer Pat Kane for his somewhat pretentious use of language. He took to social media this week to declare: 'Wean No. 2 and I laughing and crying at *Paddington* last night. But weird ideologically. Immigration references obvious, but liberal middle-class is near sanctified here and Daddy Brown clearly involved in financial innovation that unravels the very social pluralism they proclaim.'

Understandably, someone had to comment: 'Mate, it's a film about a talking bear.'

WE liked the brutal honesty of Castlemilk singer/songwriter Gerry Cinnamon whose shows are selling out fast because of a recent surge in popularity. He has told fans:

'If you're selling my tickets and you're sound, please resell them on the Twickets app at face value. If you're an old-school tout outside the show making a £20 skin, then do what you do. If you're selling tickets for two to three hundred pounds, do me a favour and only sell them in person so people can meet you and punch your face in.'

AUSTRALIAN singer Nick Cave of Bad Seeds fame was on a tour of Britain where he invited questions from the audience about his career. Best enquiry one night we reckon was the chap who asked: 'Hi, Nick. I live in your old flat in Hove. Do you know where the stopcock is?'

RACONTEUR Gyles Brandreth told the Diary of appearing on telly show *Countdown*, and going into the dressing room of the late, lamented Richard Whiteley who told him there was a hole in the wall through which you could see into Carol Vorderman's dressing room.

Then Richard added, after pausing for effect: 'I was going to call maintenance and get it mended, but then I thought, What the hell? Let her look.'

READER Andy Moffat from Rutherglen was at the excellent Bob Dylan concert in Glasgow.

But not all fans appreciated, he tells us, the fact that Bob sang a lot of his newer material rather than just playing safe by trotting out his greatest hits. Finally, one exasperated fan shouted: 'Hey, Jimmy! Do you know any Bob Dylan songs?'

FORMER Yes keyboard player Rick Wakeman at the Edinburgh Book Festival to talk about his biography, *Grumpy*

Old Rockstar, recalled a book signing where a fan informed him that he'd signed a pair of her knickers twenty years ago, and then politely asked him whether he would mind doing so again, for old times' sake.

Rick was slightly taken aback when, instead of simply taking a pair out of her bag, she asked that he sign while she was wearing them.

As he did so he heard a more elderly lady further down the queue mutter to her pal: 'Oh Flora, I do hope we don't have to do that.'

GLASTONBURY Festival, that grand-daddy of all outdoor music festivals, last weekend included Auchtermuchty legends, The Proclaimers. When Proclaimer Charlie was asked whether he would invite strangers into his back garden to drink excessively, play loud music and piddle recklessly, like Glastonbury Festival founder Michael Eavis does, he replied: 'It's a bit like that when my wife's family come to visit from Glasgow, to be honest.'

A BBC FOUR programme called *It's Time to Go Nationwide*, celebrated the old teatime telly magazine programme *Nationwide*, which reminded Glasgow-based former BBC man John Thompson of when he worked on the show in the early 1980s.

A film of a skateboarding duck was big hit on the programme, so the hunt was on to find other unusual ducks.

When a farmer in Norfolk phoned to say he had the oldest duck in Britain, a film crew rushed to his farm only, says John, to career into the farmyard, drive straight over the aforementioned duck and flatten it.

ENTERTAINER Rory Bremner, speaking at the opening of the rebranded Dunblane Hydro, now a Doubletree hotel after a multi-million-pound refurbishment, said he had recently been at a function with easyJet founder Stelios Haji-Ioannou.

'Afterwards we shared a taxi,' said Rory. 'Stelios opened the door and said, "After you."

'He then charged me £10 for priority boarding.'

WHILE in Glasgow for a show at Hampden, Sir Paul McCartney was jogging through Glasgow Green when he called in at the Winter Gardens for a cuppa.

When he said 'Hello, Samantha' to one of the Encore catering ladies – fortunately he didn't actually burst into singing the Cliff Richard song – the star-struck lady asked how he knew her name.

'I'm a qualified clairvoyant,' he replied – then pointed at her name badge.

VIDAL Sassoon, the celebrity hairdresser who died in 2012, acknowledged the style of Glasgow women by opening one of his salons in Princes Square in the city. It reminds us of when award-winning Glasgow hairdresser Rita Rusk employed Sharleen Spiteri, now singer with multi-million album selling band Texas, as a stylist, and Sharleen came to her to say that she was resigning in order to pursue a career in music. Rita admits she dismissed such a fanciful claim and accused her of covering up the fact that she was moving to Vidal Sassoon.

A BBC Scotland reporter once told us she managed to read the name of the late North Korea leader Kim Jong-il when he died without mispronouncing it. So what, you might think, but she tells us of a fellow broadcaster who read the name out as Kim Jong the Second.

OUR mention of a radio contest reminds David Macleod: 'Do you remember in the days when you had to send your answers in by post? Radio Clyde asked which pop superstar had the real name Marie McDonald McLaughlin Lawrie? The answer had to be sent to "Radio Clyde, Lulu Competition, P.O Box…"'

FORMER Central Hotel page boy Desmond Lynn tells in the sumptuous history of the hotel, *Glasgow's Grand Central Hotel* by Bill Hicks and Jill Scott, of comedy duo Laurel and Hardy staying there and waving to the thousands of fans thronging Hope Street.

Oliver Hardy asked for a pen or pencil to sign autographs,

and Desmond handed him his pencil. When Oliver remarked on how small the pencil was, Desmond boldly replied: 'Not as small as your sixpenny tip.'

The duo laughed, took the hint and handed Desmond a princely five shillings each.

RODDY Frame of Aztec Camera fame took the crowd at Glasgow's Concert Hall back to 1983 in order to play tracks from his debut album that came out all those years ago. To help the crowd, who were all of a certain age, to get in the mood of the early 1980s, Roddy told them: 'Sit back and think about the one you love; not the one you're with tonight who you're not too keen on.'

THE late Scots author William McIlvanney once told of meeting actor Sean Connery at a Scotland match at Hampden. 'I can't believe I'm here,' Connery tells him. 'I was sitting in Tramp's at two o'clock this morning when Rod Stewart walks in. He's chartered a private plane and why don't I come to the game. So here I am.' Tramp's, of course, being a well-known London nightclub.

A policeman who was with McIlvanney chipped in: 'It's a small world, big yin. Ah was in a house at Muirhead at two o'clock this mornin'. It was full o' tramps as well.'

ACTOR Rupert Everett, speaking at the Edinburgh Book Festival about his big break in Glasgow in the 1970s at the Citizens Theatre, recalled the Glasgow audiences.

Said Rupert: 'Provided the play ended at 10:20 when the last bus left, the audience really enjoyed themselves. However, if the show ran on even a minute late, the audience would still get up at 10:20 – and you could hear the clatter, clatter, clatter of their seats as they left.'

CELEBRITY encounters continued. The late Guy Robertson, boss of Guy Robertson Advertising in Glasgow, once told us:

'I took a very proper lady from an Edinburgh law firm to a sports dinner and she was seated next to boxer Frank Bruno. As she had arrived after the formal introductions, I told her it was comedian Lenny Henry.

'She chatted away oblivious, then asked, "Mr Henry, could you please do that 'Know What I Mean 'Arry' impersonation of that boxer?"

'To his credit Frank just went ahead and did it. It was only later in the evening when the MC name-checked him that she realised.'

READERS were recalling the old Apollo in Glasgow, and one told us: 'I was in the chip shop next door to the old Apollo standing beside the legendary jazz guitarist John McLaughlin who was appearing that evening. John was leaning over the counter and asking a member of staff slowly and incredulously, "You FRY the pizza?"'

LACONIC former accountant Arnold Brown, widely regarded as the godfather of alternative comedy, received a lifetime achievement award at the Scottish Comedy Awards. We liked his reaction to getting the award.

'It's always been great to be regarded as the comedian's comedian,' he said, 'but my real ambition has always been to be the bank manager's comedian.'

WE liked the interview with Boothby Graffoe on the Glasgow comedy club The Stand's website in which he is asked about his show *Scratch!*, about lotteries and scratchcards.

Asked: 'What research did you do?' he replied: 'I looked at the socioeconomic effects of the lottery. It's disheartening when you realise that, despite the charitable benefits, there is a terrible greed underpinning the entire concept. With this show I'm hoping to make people see that if they win a lot of money then the greatest thing they could do with it is to help other people.'

'If you were to win big, would you continue with the tour?'

'You wouldn't see me for dust.'

JOHN Fisher's book on British comedians, *Funny Way To Be A Hero*, recounts how Edinburgh's Ronnie Corbett met his future stage partner Ronnie Barker when Corbett was working between jobs as a barman in a London club for actors. Because of his lack of inches there were two crates behind the bar which he stood on, one with the name Agnes and the other with the name Champ.

It was only when Barker asked him who Agnes was that Corbett explained it was a crate marked Champagnes that had been sawn in half.

A POLITICIAN who lives in Blackburn, the same village as *Britain's Got Talent* singing sensation Susan Boyle, tells us the story going around the village is that two smartly suited chaps were seen wandering around the area before going in to a local pub. Looking around, they asked the barmaid why the pub was so empty.

When she asked where they were from, they said American television company CBS, wanting to do a piece on Susan.

'CBS!' she told them. 'We thought you were DSS, which is why everyone bailed.'

GLASGOW-BORN author Ryan O'Neill, now living in Australia, tells us: 'I've been in Australia about thirteen years, but as Australians never tire of telling me, I still have my Glaswegian accent.

'In a shop the assistant asked me, "Anything else?" and I said, "No thanks, that's all." After we walked out, my friend who was with me said in a shocked voice, "Why did you call him an asshole?"'

RETIRED *Daily Record* journalist Jim Davis recalls that he was once sent to a charity golf event at Renfrew to interview volatile racing driver James Hunt. Says Jim:

'*The Record* had got phone calls from readers complaining about Hunt wearing grubby jeans and T-shirt with one describing him as, "Lookin' as if he's jist fell oot a midden. The weans ur getting a right bad example set here, so they urr."

'Hunt was in the bar beside an immaculate Sean Connery, Henry Cooper and Dickie Henderson. I got out: "Mr Hunt, our *Daily Record* readers are complaining that your appearance is downright scruffy. And they say you're setting a bad example to the kids. What's your response?"

'His memorable reply in a cut-glass accent was, "You can tell your readers that they are confusing me with someone who actually gives a ****."'

MEMORIES of American singing star Johnny Cash's visits to Glasgow, with an usher in the old Green's Playhouse telling us when Cash had two shows on the same day.

He said: 'As the man in black entered from the wings he tripped on a trailing cable and drawled: "Who put that darned thing thar?" to much amusement.

'Ever the showman, Johnny decided to keep it in the act and amazingly tripped at the exact same spot at the second show that evening.'

AS more TV and film productions are shot in Scotland, an actor chum who had a minor role in the hugely successful Jacobite romp *Outlander* tells us: 'Filming in Scotland's worst weather was harsh. At one point the director ordered a few of us dressed as Highlanders to take a couple of horses and be silhouetted on a hill in the driving rain while they filmed.

'After a while, though, we saw a couple of helpers, on the say-so of the director who had halted filming, struggling up the hill carrying blankets.

'That cheered us up – until they finally arrived and put them over the horses.'

12

Keeping It in the Family

When the generations collide at home, the outcome can often be hilarious.

A FATHER managed to keep his face straight when his teenage daughter was pleading to have a pony, and her mother, claiming it was too expensive, told her that the pony would need new shoes every six weeks.

'No different from you, then, Mum,' replied the feisty teenager.

A CHAP in Milngavie phoned his widowed mum to see how she was, not knowing she had bought some flower bulbs at the supermarket that day which she wanted to plant on her husband's grave.

So you can imagine his shock when she told him: 'Bring a

spade when you come at the weekend. We're going to visit your dad.'

THE impending onslaught of Christmas shopping reminds us of the harassed woman wrapping a late Christmas present for one of her daughter's friends, when her little girl pointed out as she finished that the wrapping paper was printed with 'Happy Birthday'.

'Just write Jesus below it,' said her exasperated mum.

'MY daughter,' said the woman having coffee with friends in Edinburgh this week, 'has just texted saying "call me ASAP".'

'I think,' she told her friends, 'I'll just stick to Jennifer.'

A WEST END reader overhears a Sauvignon-swilling woman in an Ashton Lane bar musing on the passage of time. 'You know you're getting old,' she told the folk with her, 'when your friends start having kids on purpose.'

DOUGLAS McLeod in Newlands, Glasgow, recalls a friend's five-year-old daughter visiting her grandmother who had no sweets in the house and instead gave the child an oatcake covered with jam as a treat.

A few minutes later the little girl appeared back in the kitchen with the uneaten oatcake on the plate, now minus the jam, and announced: 'Thanks for the jam, Granny – and here's your wee board back.'

A YOUNG lad in Govan told his mum if she paid him a quid, he'd be good for the rest of the day. 'I shouldn't have to pay you to be good,' his mother replied. 'You should be good for nothin' – just like yer faither.'

GLASGOW stand-up Larry Dean told of sitting his mum and dad down in the kitchen and telling them he was gay. 'My father stormed out of the room,' recalled Larry. 'I was standing there thinking I had ruined the family and how would we recover from this when he came back in and handed my mum a tenner.'

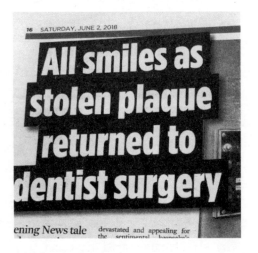

16 SATURDAY, JUNE 2, 2018

All smiles as stolen plaque returned to dentist surgery

ening News tale devastated and appealing for
the sentimental keepsake's

A READER in Hyndland was impressed that his teenage daughter was trying a simple crossword in a magazine until she asked:

'How many letters does "toast" have?'

When he confirmed it was of course five, her face fell, as

the word she was looking for had only four. 'What's the clue?' he asked.

'Egg on,' she replied.

YOUNG Scottish comedian Daniel Sloss told of the fun he and his younger brother had when they went on holiday with their parents.

Daniel said: 'As soon as our dad started taking his belt off to go through the security scanner at the airport we would look alarmed and shout out: "No, Dad! I'm sorry!"'

SOME of you might look back to your youth and identify with the twenty-year-old girl, Lizzie, who admitted on social media this week: 'Told my dad I ran out of alcohol and didn't have any money to buy any for the weekend . . . so he gave me the huge bottle of vodka from the cupboard that I stole and replaced with water when I was sixteen. Life really does come back to bite you on the backside.'

WE remember one Glasgow reader who realised his son, going into Primary 6, was getting older when he stopped him at the door and said he wanted to take his picture, as he has done on previous years. But this time his son just brushed past him, held up his hand, and said: 'Not a good time.'

A PAISLEY reader was in the Braehead shopping centre where he watched a harassed mother dealing with a gurning young boy who was constantly seeking her attention. Eventually she snapped at him: 'Go and play with your wee brother. That's what we had him for.'

SO, did you hear about the young lad who went home and told his parents he had bought a theatre?

'Are you having me on?' declared his mum.

'Well, I'll give you an audition, but I'm not promising anything,' he told her.

A GLASGOW mother who had been out shopping all day had left her son at her sister's. When she arrived to collect him, the little lad told her proudly: 'I've been a good boy today.'

'You can't get into much trouble lying on the couch all day,' his aunt explained.

'Dad does,' the little one replied.

A READER looking over his son's Modern Studies Higher paper was reminded of his own days at school when he had a project on the Second World War. He interviewed his own father and, as he tells us: 'I reached the point where I felt I had to ask, in a somewhat quiet voice, whether he had ever killed anyone. My dad answered in an equally quiet voice, "Probably. I was a cook for some time."'

A CHAP in an Ayrshire golf club was heard to argue: 'My children had the cheek to say I need to go to anger management classes. I told them I didn't need anger management, I just needed people to stop irritating me.'

A BEARSDEN reader emails us: 'I was so distracted in the kitchen at the weekend that I asked my dog to hand me something. To be fair, he gave me the same blank stare my children would have.'

A READER confesses to us: 'Based on the things my children will and won't eat, my cooking is apparently worse than a Polo mint found on the floor with dog hair on it.'

A MERRYLEE father tells us: 'My son has just passed his driving test and on Saturday he texted me, "Can I borrow the car later?" I thought I was quite clever when I texted back, "Of course you can! But that's not how you spell 'wash'."'

AN Edinburgh reader was leaving his home when he noticed the girl in the flat opposite open her front door while still talking on her house cordless phone.

He was about to tell her that such phones don't work far from the base unit when she stopped outside her open door and rang her front-door bell.

His mystification was cleared up when he then heard her say on the phone: 'I'll have to go, Mum. That's someone at the front door.'

A READER tells us he took his family for a special meal at a country-house hotel which had mounted stags' heads in the foyer. One of them had a couple of party hats hanging from its antlers.

Noticing his young daughter had stopped walking and was staring at the head, he told her that unfortunately some folk liked to hunt animals.

'But why did they have to shoot him on his birthday?' she wailed.

A READER in Knightswood, Glasgow, out for a stroll in the good weather, sees a child attempting to manoeuvre the family lawnmower which had been left out in the garden.

The child's mother spots him and shouts something our reader agrees is very true: 'If that mower cuts aff yer toes, don't come running to me.'

READER Norman Brown in Barassie tells us of a friend who was asked by his five-year-old son: 'Daddy, what does baws mean?' The shocked parent replied that it was not a very nice word, he was never to say it again and, anyway, where had he heard it?

'Mummy,' his son replied. 'Every night she says it's time for beddy-baws.'

OUR story about a stroppy kid in the supermarket reminded reader David Macleod of telling his then six-year-old son off for bad behaviour and adding:

'Right – that's it! No McDonald's for you today.'

They walked on in silence for a while before his son piped up: 'Dad, see instead of not going to McDonald's – can I not go to the Thistle game instead?'

A MUM was impressed by the manners of the little girl who arrived at her daughter's sixth birthday party and chirruped as she came in the door: 'In case I forget, I'd like to say that I had a very nice time.'

A PART-TIME worker in Boots tells us about a customer leaving his mobile phone on the counter. So she scrolled through the saved numbers, stopped at 'Mum' and phoned the woman to tell her that her son had left his phone in the shop.

'Don't worry,' said the mum, 'I'll take care of it.'

Two minutes later, the mobile rang and the assistant couldn't stop herself from answering, to hear a woman's voice: 'Martin. You've gone and left your phone in Boots.'

WEST of Scotland men have always had difficulty showing their emotion. One young lad having a beer with his pals in Glasgow's West End on Friday declared: 'The only time I could get a hug from my dad was when I pretended to choke so that he would try the Heimlich manoeuvre on me.'

A NEWTON MEARNS reader confides to us she was putting face cream on when her little son asked why she was doing it.

'To make myself look beautiful,' she replied.

Minutes later when she was removing the cream, her little one, who had not stopped staring at her, asked: 'Giving up?'

AN Edinburgh reader swears that a chap having coffee in Starbucks told the business acquaintance with him: 'I'm such an idiot. I forgot my sister's birthday last week.'

His friend tried to reassure him that it was not an uncommon slip-up, but the chap then added: 'But we're twins.'

WE were discussing the age-old problem of how to keep children amused with prominent Glasgow lawyer Austin Lafferty, who told us that his wife was having a cup of tea in the vast Silverburn shopping centre when a big Glasgow family commandeered the next table.

Said Austin: 'The children were obstreperous, especially one young girl who was shouting the odds and running around to everyone's annoyance.

'Eventually her mother, hard-pressed with a babe in arms also squalling, had a brainwave, and asked the wee girl, "Haw, Abigail, want tae come and watch me wipe yer sister's arse?"'

OUR story about television remote controls reminds Jim Scott of earlier days when folk had their makeshift alternatives. 'When I was at school my pal's dad had a snooker cue with another bit of wood taped to it which he used to push the buttons on his wood-grain effect Ferguson TV. He could also use it to adjust the set-top aerial, poke the dog when it started snoring in front of the fire, and skelp us if we were making too much noise.'

HER friends looked aghast as a woman in a Glasgow coffee shop yesterday announced: 'I got home to find all the windows and doors wide open. Everything was gone. What kind of sick person would do that to another human being?' She then added: 'I knew I shouldn't have left the kids' advent calendars where my husband could get at them.'

WE hear from Kilwinning in Ayrshire where a local lady has had to cancel her plans for a lavish fiftieth birthday party. It was pointed out to her that having it just four months after her parents' equally lavish Golden Wedding anniversary celebrations might raise an eyebrow or two amongst the more numerate.

SAYS Dougie McNicol: 'A friend on a visit to his son and daughter-in-law asked if they had a newspaper. "Dad," scoffed the son, "this is the twenty-first century. We don't do newspapers. Use my iPad."

'Say what you like about new technology,' the friend later told Dougie. 'That fly never knew what hit it!'

AH, the generation gap. A Milngavie reader realised her grandson had never seen loose tea leaves because the family always used tea bags. 'Fortune tellers used to read tea leaves,' she told him in a bout of reminiscing.

'I didn't even know you could write on them,' he told her.

DADS who think they're funny, continued. A young Lanarkshire girl was keen to have some pet goldfish, so while searching the cupboard she shouted out:

'Have you seen the fish bowl?'

'No,' shouted back Dad, 'but I think I saw the cat playing darts once.'

THE minister at Motherwell South Church was introducing the story of Samson and Delilah to the children in the congregation and, trying to involve them as much as possible, she asked: 'What do you know about Samson?'

Alas, the story of the hair cut didn't immediately come to mind with one young lad who, trying to remember where he thought he had seen the name before, put up his hand and shouted:

'He made oor telly, miss.'

GLASGOW comedian Raymond Mearns once explained that his teenage daughter thought he drove a 'magic taxi'.

'Not only,' said Raymond, 'did she expect it to take her from the house to anywhere she wanted to go to in Glasgow, but at the end of the journey I had to hand her a tenner instead of the other way round.'

A BOTHWELL reader recalled when folk had to send telegrams to wish relatives abroad a Good New Year. An old uncle in Dumfries some years ago sent such a message to his sister in Canada which ended with the traditional New Year greeting 'Lang May Your Lum Reek'.

She still has it framed on her wall as along the way it was typed up and sent as 'Lang May Your Bum Reek'.

A BEARSDEN reader tells us that last summer his grand-daughter raced in to tell him that there were a large number of snails on the garden path. Thinking of a well-known remedy, our reader announced: 'I'll get some salt.'

'You're not going to eat them?' screeched a horrified grand-daughter.

KINSHIP Care which helps family members, often grand-parents, who bring up children was told by one couple: 'When our grand-daughter first came to stay with us she told social workers we had given her bones for her tea. It was actually spare ribs.'

A CLARKSTON reader tells us she caught her four-year-old daughter lifting some grapes from her younger sister's plate. 'Are you stealing your sister's grapes?' demanded mum.

'No,' she replied. 'I'm teaching her to share.'

A SOUTHSIDE reader tells us she had her two young grandsons staying over at Easter while their parents had a break. She had put the boys to bed, and had gone for a shower when she heard them noisily jumping around the room. With her make-up off, clad in a dressing gown and her hair bundled into a towel, she stormed into their room and told them to get to sleep. As she left the room she heard one of the boys whisper: 'Who was that?'

A GLASGOW reader tells us about her group of girlfriends meeting up. One of them, a mother of four, was asked, if she had her time again, would she still have four children?

'Absolutely,' she replied. 'Just not the same ones.'

A CHAP in a Glasgow pub was being asked how his teenage son was.

'It's the golden year,' he replied.

'What's that?' he was asked.

'It's the year when he's old enough not to need a babysitter, but too young to borrow my car,' he replied.

EVER had a rubbish birthday? Jake Lambert passes on to us: 'The night before my friend's seventeenth birthday, his brother borrowed his friend's new car, put a ribbon in it and parked it in their driveway.'

'DO you know what's fun?' a cyclist phones to tell us. 'Riding one of those bikes with a toddler seat at the back with no one in it and saying very loudly when you pass folk on the street, "You're being very well behaved today."'

ON, for some unknown reason, National Biscuit Day, a reader recalled: 'Do you remember the thrill when you went home as a lad and found a biscuit tin on the kitchen table, and you eagerly opened it up hoping to wolf down a Bourbon or a Custard Cream only to discover your ma's sewing kit?'

GLASGOW Airport was attempting to reunite owners with their lost teddy bears that had accumulated at the airport. It reminded a Glasgow reader that years ago a neighbour gave his young daughter an enormous pink teddy bear for her birthday, but he was not keen on it as it was stuffed with polystyrene spheres that he felt could be a choking hazard.

His solution was to quietly slip it into the bin, hoping the neighbour would not ask about it. His guile, alas, was undone the following week when the bin lorry roared into the street with said pink bear tied to the front grille.

A LANARKSHIRE reader tells us he was at the Golden Wedding celebrations of an old friend in a local hotel when the couple's son stood up and made an emotional speech about how much his parents meant to him and ended it with: 'Thank you for having such a lovely marriage.'

The man's father piped up: 'And thank you for making it necessary.'

13

It's All Politics

There seems to have been a heck of a lot of politics recently. Fortunately our readers spotted a few of the lighter moments.

WHEN Boris Johnson became Prime Minister we recalled former PM David Cameron telling a Westminster Correspondents' Dinner: 'I remember canvassing in a South Hampstead suburb with Boris during the London Mayoral election and this very attractive middle-aged woman came to the door and said, "Boris! Lovely to see you! You are the father of one of my children!"

'The white hair stood on end. He said, "Oh God, oh cripes, oh. The media! What do you want? Is it money?"

'She said, "No, you are the father of one of my children! I'm her maths teacher."'

CAT lovers will understand what the Scottish Health Minister Jeane Freeman did while others will just shake their heads in disbelief. We simply pass on a magazine interview with Jeane when she mentioned her dear departed pet cat Tosca and was asked what the most ridiculous thing was she had ever done for her pet.

Jeane replied: 'We headbutted a cat-flap. It took Tosca six months to work out the cat-flap – it was only after many weeks of personal demonstrations that she caught on.'

NOT much fun in Brexit, but as Glasgow stand-up Janey Godley explained: 'At last night's show in Edinburgh a woman from the Netherlands in the front row agreed to post me over insulin and migraine tablets. So, in seven seconds I got a better Brexit deal than the Tory government did in two years.'

RETIRED Maryhill Labour MP Maria Fyfe told in her autobiography, *A Problem Like Maria*, of a Glasgow MP who wanted to send a letter to the blind government minister David Blunkett, and went to the trouble of having it put into Braille.

Well done we say. However, when he got the Braille copy back, he then faxed it.

SHE also recalled Tory grandee Nicholas Soames, grandson of Winston Churchill, standing for election in Clydebank. His cause wasn't helped by the SNP publishing a photo of him winning a polo match, holding aloft the trophy brimming with champagne, his horse on one side, a blonde beauty on the other.

Knocking doors in Clydebank, Nicholas was finding little support until in one multi-storey, a chap said he would vote Conservative. Astonished, Nicholas asked him why and he replied: 'Any man who likes horses, booze and women can't be all bad.'

AFTER a Queen's Speech in Parliament, a political contact called to say: 'The thing about the public's perception of the

Tories these days is that when the Queen's speech includes a Modern Slavery Bill you have to stop to think whether the government is opposing it or bringing it in.'

FORMER Tory leader David Cameron, on a visit to Scotland when Gordon Brown was Prime Minister, told party members that he had written to Gordon asking if he had any objections to him touring his Kirkcaldy constituency and talking to the voters.

The PM, said Cameron, had merely replied with a curt 'No, you can't.'

'Mind you,' added the Tory leader, 'it was the strangest spelling of can't that I'd seen.'

COUNCILS across Scotland are sent requests for information under the Freedom of Information Act from numerous newspapers looking for stories. We hear about one council which was asked by a newspaper:

'What is the oddest FOI question you've been asked?'

The council just had to reply: 'This one.'

WE liked losing Labour MP in East Kilbride Michael McCann's quick adjustment to his new status after his seat was taken by the SNP.

When asked by BBC reporter Catriona Renton for an interview after he was defeated, he crisply replied: 'I don't need to talk to you, I'm not a politician anymore.'

FORMER Ayrshire Labour MP Brian Donohoe told us of Deputy Speaker Harold Walker delivering leaflets at an election shortly after a Tory canvasser had been too lazy to push the Tory leaflets right through the letterbox, so Harold would take them out and stuff them in his pocket.

Disaster struck when he arrived at one door and, looking round, realised that he had walked through the wet cement of a newly laid driveway. Harold quickly took a Tory leaflet out of his pocket, shoved it through the letterbox and made his escape.

SOMETIMES you have to praise the honesty of politicians. At one election, the Tory candidate in Motherwell was asked in a local youth magazine interview, along with all the other candidates, what his links were with the town. He replied: 'Have seen Motherwell Football Club playing on *Sportscene*.'

A POSTSCRIPT to former president Bill Clinton's speaking engagement in Glasgow, and his round of golf at Prestwick beforehand. Local caddy Buff, who carried Clinton's bag, was asked if he had called him 'Bill' or 'Mr President'.

'Ah, well, all the way round the course,' said Buff, 'it was Bill. But when he gave me a $200 tip at the end, then it was Mr President.'

WE asked for your memories of the boozy business lunches of yore, and John Crawford tell us: 'Many years ago my mate sold refuse collection vehicles, and had to entertain a left-wing council leader to lunch after receiving a good order. On being offered the wine list, the councillor chose a bottle each of the most expensive red and white wines, poured himself half a glass of each, then shouted "corks".

'The waiters, obviously used to this, brought him the corks which he forced into the bottles, stuck one in each jacket pocket then ordered two pints of lager.'

ACTOR and comedian Des McLean lost ten pounds in order to appear as maverick politician Tommy Sheridan in Ian Pattison's black comedy *I, Tommy* at Glasgow's King's Theatre. To achieve that, the once chubby-cheeked impersonator hired a personal trainer who dragged him through the pain barrier exercising every day.

'There were times,' says Des, 'when I wished it was Alex

Salmond I was playing instead, as I would then have an excuse to go on the kebabs all week to get the right look.'

WHO could fail to be a fan of Scottish eloquence?

A Cumbernauld reader once told us: 'My daughter was listening to a news item on Spanish television about the local elections in the UK. The only Scot interviewed said he was not going to vote, and when asked why, he replied that the parties "are two cheeks of the same bum".'

OUR former *Evening Times* colleague, political reporter Ian Hernon, once told us of a Labour conference where the Glasgow trade unionist chairing the session was trying to pick out the next speaker from the delegates holding their hands up. He managed to either horrify or amuse those present by declaring: 'That lassie in the red frock. No, not you hen, the pretty one in the next row.'

READERS who occasionally have to make speeches in public will feel sympathy for Bailie Phil Greene of Glasgow City Council who revealed, at the opening reception of the Glasgow International Comedy Festival, that his wife was not with him. He explained: 'She said to me, "You'll tell a joke, it will fall flat and I'll be embarrassed. So I'm not going."'

But actually Phil did make us laugh in an ironic way. He apologised for being late as the Lord Provost's limo was sent to collect him – and it got a flat tyre thumping into one of the potholes on the road that the council is supposed to maintain.

THE late Tony Benn introduced a film about his career at Celtic Connections in Glasgow and told of driving near Westminster many years ago when he had an urgent need to go to the loo. In desperation he lifted the bonnet of the car, and relieved himself over the engine, hoping he would be out of public sight.

However a passer-by stopped and told him: 'I see your problem – your radiator's leaking.'

TALES of Labour Party membership reminded John Henderson: 'In the late 1980s when I was the Labour agent in affluent Bath, Ken Loach, the left-wing filmmaker of *Cathy Come Home* fame, decided to hold a press conference to renounce his party membership, as he felt Neil Kinnock was moving the party too much to the centre.

'The trouble was, I had to inform Loach and the press that it was a bit difficult for me to react to him leaving because, despite several written reminders, he hadn't paid his membership fees for three years, so technically he didn't have a membership to renounce.'

GLASGOW stand-up Janey Godley received much publicity for holding up a very rude sign when Donald Trump last visited Scotland. It contained a word not used in respectable society.

Anyway, Janey has revealed: 'Two Tories in my comedy gig tonight. Man smugly shouts, "I hear you swear a lot. What's your worst word? Go on let me hear it. We all know you are famous for saying it." I reply, "Foodbanks." Audience cheers. Man sits raging.'

14

Just the Ticket

In happier times, public transport gave our readers a wealth of material.

JAMIE Stewart was on a bus in the West End's Byres Road when a rough-looking chap boarded and sat beside a rather posh elderly lady from Kelvinside in the seats reserved for the elderly and infirm.

Minutes later the jaikie broke wind so loudly it could be heard by all the passengers.

'Don't worry, hen,' he turned and told the shocked Kelvinside lady. 'They'll probably think it was me.'

The bus was in such an uproar the poor woman got off at the next stop.

A READER tells us about getting a train home when a little girl with her dad watched a chap being a bit unsteady on his feet.

'He's probably had too many beers,' said her dad.

But the little girl replied: 'Rachel's daddy likes beer.'

So her dad explained: 'Yes, but if you have too many it can make you fall over.'

'Should we tell Rachel's daddy?' said the girl.

'Oh, he probably knows,' replied her dad.

WE are not that gullible, surely, but a Paisley reader told us that a bus was holding up traffic in Glasgow's Hope Street while it stopped at the lights with its hazard flashers on. The driver, in the pouring rain, was out of his cab, trying to fix his broken windscreen wipers.

A woman driver pulled up beside him, felt sorry for him in the rain, rolled down her window and asked: 'Excuse me, would you like a screwdriver?'

Without missing a beat, he replied: 'Thanks for the offer, hen, but I'm running ten minutes late as it is.'

WE pass on the urban legend of the chap replacing a six-foot-long fluorescent strip light in his kitchen, who was told that the dustmen wouldn't take away the dud tube, and so he decided to take it to work to leave in his company's large bins.

Getting on the underground, he noticed the carriage becoming increasingly busy, so he held the light up above his head. However, two other passengers who squeezed on thought it was a handrail and held on at either end.

At the next stop, the chap simply got off, leaving them with the dud strip light.

A BRIDGE OF WEIR reader lost one of her shoes on the bus. No, it was not a drunken night out, but the fact that she has dressier shoes she wears at work, which she carries in a bag, and one of them had fallen out without her noticing.

After phoning the bus company, she was delighted to discover it had been handed in, and hubby was dispatched to the bus depot to collect it. When he entered the office and explained his mission, the chap behind the counter called to the back office: 'Wullie, that's Cinderella's man here!'

A NUMBER of Glasgow bus stops now have electronic displays showing when the next bus is due to arrive. Reader Dougie Lyden was reading such a display on Maryhill Road, which informed him that three buses were due in the next ten minutes, when an aged sage next to him declared: 'Ah widnae pay too much heed tae that, son. They bus stoaps are famous for talkin' a loada s***e.'

A GLASGOW reader heard an auld fella on his bus into town discussing with his pal the current fashion to have tattoos, and he came out with the memorable line: 'I mean, when I was young you could make out what they were – a heart or a flower or something. But now some o' they young folks' arms look like the inside of your old school desk's lid.'

THE Italian newspaper *La Stampa* was writing about Glasgow, with the Italian reporter arriving at Central Station and calling an Uber taxi. The driver told him that he had been an airport driver for twenty years but had been told by a pal about this new thing called Uber. He feared that it would ruin the taxi trade so he sold his licence just before Uber arrived here. When the Italian visitor asked who he had sold the licence to, he laughed and replied: 'The brother-in-law.'

A FEMALE reader tells us: 'It's pretty obvious that car designers are all men. Why isn't there a button on the dash-board you can press for "it's only some shopping bags, for God's sake" when the fasten seat-belt pinger goes off?'

AH, public transport at the festive season. Nicki on social media declares: 'You don't know what fun is until you've witnessed a drunk on the Edinburgh to Glasgow train screaming, "Ah hate hedgehogs – come at me, ya jabby wee ****!" while angrily circling a hairbrush that's been dropped on the floor.'

A READER claims that a well-dressed woman got on the train to Glasgow at Helensburgh with a youngster, obviously her grandson, and buried her face in a magazine while he looked out of the window. After the train had trundled eastwards for a while, the little one asked: 'Where are we?'

Without looking up she told him: 'I don't know, Justin. But it won't be anywhere nice.'

A LANARK reader driving his family to visit relatives in Devon couldn't believe it when one of his youngsters asked soon into the journey the inevitable: 'Are we nearly there yet?' He tried to nip this line of questioning in the bud by telling his kids that they wouldn't reach their destination until after it was dark. His hopes of a question-free journey were dashed when his youngster asked shortly afterwards: 'Is is nearly dark yet?'

IRISH government minister Dinny McGinley tells us that as a student he took the boat over from Ireland and secured a summer job as a clippie on Glasgow's trolley buses.

Years later Ireland's infamous Taoiseach, Charles Haughey, boasted about being the first politician to introduce free travel on buses. Dinny interrupted him and said: 'I think you'll find

I introduced free travel on Glasgow's trolley buses whenever I heard a Donegal accent.'

READER Brenda Gillies was on the inaugural flight from Dundee to Belfast and, to celebrate the event, the stewardess asked: 'Would youse like a glass of Buckfast?'

Says Brenda: 'When I suggested she perhaps meant bucks fizz, given the orange juice/cava combo on offer, the reply came, "Oh s***, so I do." Ah, the glamour of domestic flight.'

POLITICAL activist and comedian Mark Thomas was in Glasgow performing at Oran Mor. We can all feel his pain as he tweeted from his train heading south the next day: 'Teens playing Beyoncé through mini speakers on train. Tempted to dance in the aisle next to them shouting, "I love this one!"'

A READER on the bus into Glasgow this week heard a young chap discuss with a pal a visit to a city centre club at the weekend. 'A girl at the bar asked me if I thought she had too much make-up on,' he recounted.

'I told her it depends on whether she was wanting to kill Batman or not.'

NIGEL Manuel recalled taking his Auntie Maisie over to Dunoon on Western Ferries. He told us: 'The ticket guy came to the car and quoted me £19 as the price. Auntie, previously unnoticed in the back seat, pipes up that as a senior citizen she is entitled to a discount. "That'll be twenty-five quid then," said the ticket collector giving the revised price now that he had spotted my aunt.'

FIFE WORLD CUP LIVE 2014, 8.30pm: Coverage of the second quarter final between Brazil and Colombia.

BUS drivers in the city are told not to stop for anyone who is not at a bus stop. But a reader tells us he was on a night bus in Glasgow when the driver, obviously feeling sorry for the chap on a cold night, stopped for a passenger gently swaying on the pavement who held out his hand in between stops. He wished he hadn't bothered when he opened the doors and the chap merely inquired: 'Huv ye goat a light?'

A YOUNG girl on the 66 bus in Glasgow was telling her pal that she got a 'big riddy' at the weekend when she saw a chap bending down and picking up fag ends from the street. As she explained: 'Ma heart went out to him, so broke he had to smoke fag ends, so I handed him a couple of cigarettes from my packet.

'That's when he told me he worked in the shop and had been sent out to sweep up.'

A RETIRED Glasgow bus driver told us of the female passenger at the bus stop who shouted in to him: 'Can you wait, driver, until I get my clothes on?'

He tells us all his other passengers were straining their necks for a look until they realised she was merely humphing two big bags from the laundrette next to the stop.

A READER on the Edinburgh to Glasgow train noted three raucous women on board, encumbered with shopping after, presumably, a day of retail and pinot grigio therapy. Across from them a fellow traveller's phone rang and he was heard telling the caller that yes, he knew he should have been home by then but he had to work late at the office, and no, he had not gone for a drink after work, and no, he had not gone for a drink with the new receptionist.

The demeanour of the chap on the phone, says our reader, was not helped by one of the ladies opposite, when he denied having a drink with the receptionist, shouting across: 'Put that phone down and come back to bed.'

A QUEUE formed at coffee shop Starbucks at Glasgow's Queen Street station last week when the company held their giveaway promotion 'A free latte with your name on it.'

Reader Frank Murphy reports: 'The queue cracked up when the barista holding a felt tip pen to write on the cup asked their next customer: "What's your name?"

'Shouting from further back in the queue was a fan of Dad's Army who declared: "Don't tell him, Pike!"'

A NEWTON MEARNS reader on the train into Glasgow watched as a retired gentleman searched his pockets for his ticket when asked for it by the guard. Seeing how frantic the chap was, the ScotRail chap told him: 'It's okay. I'm sure you've got one.'

'I still need to find it,' the old chap replied. 'I've forgotten where I'm going.'

A STIRLING reader travelling by train to Edinburgh had to endure standing room only in the crowded carriage while the conductor apologised, stating: 'This is due to the school holidays and the Edinburgh Festival.'

'Which of these,' wondered our passenger to himself, 'took ScotRail by surprise?'

BAD weather meant people turning to alternative transport, and one Glasgow traveller, new to First buses, asked the Polish driver for a 'Noddy ticket'. He stared at her blankly.

So she insisted: 'I was told to ask for a Noddy ticket.' Still no response.

At that the chap behind her spoke up: 'She wants an all-day ticket.'

A FORMER driving test examiner tells us about a middle-aged driver in Ayrshire sitting her test who found the road blocked by a van of workies half-heartedly unloading scaffolding. She asked the examiner what to do and he replied, as he had to: 'Do what you would normally do in such circumstances.'

She then surprised him by getting out the car and shouting at the workmen: 'Wid youse idle b******* shift that truck tae ah get past, yer haudin' upma drivin' test.'

The truck was immediately shifted, but the lady failed her test.

GLASGOW'S Queen Street station is of course a terminus. That would seem obvious from the row of buffers facing the trains. Nevertheless Dave Martin in Dundee tells us he was catching the Glasgow to Dundee train at Queen Street when a group of American tourists came on.

One of them asked the Scottish chap across the table from him if he knew if his seat was forward facing.

'I hope not,' replied the Scot. 'Otherwise we'd be heading for George Square.'

BAD weather has been disrupting some ferry services around Scotland. But not everyone has felt the cancellations were necessary. David Kelso was at a newsagent's in Brodick, Arran, at the weekend where a sign stuck to the door stated in bright red ink: 'No papers.' Added in explanation below was: 'You may think it's not windy, I may think it's not windy, but the CalMac psychic decided yesterday at lunchtime there was a chance a seagull might fart causing a sudden gust of wind.'

A HELENSBURGH reader once told us that he and his pal in Edinburgh for the rugby thought they would get the train from Waverley to Haymarket for the game rather than walk there. It is the shortest rail journey you can take from Waverley.

When they asked for two tickets to Haymarket the ticket clerk, who had never sold a ticket to Haymarket before, asked: 'Dae yiz want tae book a sleeper?"

CATCHING a ferry to the continent reminded reader Ian Glasgow:

'I once saw a magician on a ferry where the crowd was a bit uninterested. He managed to persuade a volunteer to go up on stage and blindfold him.

'But after doing this the volunteer just walked off stage never to be seen again, leaving the magician asking thin air to "Pick a card". It was funnier than the comedian.'

READER Frank Murphy tells us about a Glasgow taxi driver who picked up a tipsy female in town after a night out. She never spoke on the journey home until they arrived and she said:

'Can I ask how the fare is £9 when it was only £2 on the way in?'

The puzzled driver argued: 'Couldn't have been £2. The meter starts at £2.40.'

'I'm telling you it was £2 each,' the girl insisted.

'Each?' replied the driver. 'How many of you were there?'

'Five.'

GLASGOW'S old sludge boats, which carried human waste out to sea, were being discussed at Jim Morrison's bowling club, where one worthy said he had worked on the SS *Dalmarnock* in the 1990s. 'Was it not a bit smelly?' he was asked.

'A bit, at times,' he replied. 'But it was a great wee number, down the Clyde in the morning, back up in the afternoon, and for some reason I always got a seat to masel going home on the bus at night.'

CATCHING the bus into Glasgow, a reader heard a young chap ask a pal he met:

'You look rough. Did you have one of your famous drunken nights?'

'No,' replied the pal. 'Sadly it was one of my not-so-famous sober nights.'

THEY can be tricky things these train toilets. As broadcaster Gyles Brandreth once related after a visit to Yorkshire:

'I was outside the WC, pressed the button, the door opened and a poor sod inside turned frantically towards me, unable to staunch his flow. As he waved his arms in alarm, his spray went everywhere.

'"Shut the door!" he cried as his trousers fell to his ankles. Then I pressed the button on the outside just as he pressed the button on the inside, so the closing door reopened – that's when he slipped.'

BUS tours are still popular, and reader John Barrington told us:

'A while ago, one of the tour bus drivers, who frequented Inversnaid Hotel, was renowned for pointing out places of interest to his passengers, mostly people from south of Hadrian's Wall.

'His particular passion seemed to be ancient battlefields; here the hillside where the Scots beat the Auld Enemy, there the field where the Scots triumphed over the Auld Enemy, And so on, day after day.

'Towards the end of one particular holiday, a visitor spoke up saying that, from his now rather distant schooldays, he could remember the teacher telling of an occasional English victory over the Scots. This met with the instant rejoinder, "No' on my bus, they didn't!"'

LATE night in Glasgow and we jump into a taxi and recognise the driver.

'Is your brother still driving your taxi during the day?' we ask.

'No, I had to sack him,' says our driver.

'Why was that?' we ask.

'Well, despite what experts say, his passengers didn't like it when he tried to go the extra mile.'

OUR favourite Glasgow Corpy bus story is the one the late, great Chic Murray told when discussing the culture of seeking compensation, that when he was a schoolboy he was on the top deck of a Corpy bus with his father when the bus performed an abrupt emergency stop.

Passengers were thrown forwards, and Chic recalled: 'I was uninjured, but fortunately my father had the presence of mind to throw me down the stairs.'

15

Good Health

Even a visit to the hospital can bring out a Scottish sense of humour.

A READER tells us he was attending a fracture clinic where he got into conversation with a chap having his leg, which was in a stookie, checked. The man said he was a former window cleaner.

Our reader asked him when he'd given up the job, which allowed the chap to give his prepared answer: 'Halfway down.'

'I WENT to the doc's,' said the chap in the pub the other night, 'with a terrible pain in my foot.'

'The first thing he said to me was, "Gout."

'But I told him, "Hang on, I've just got here."'

A CHAP whose wife was in hospital bumped into a pal who asked him how his wife was.

'Critical,' he replied.

His shocked pal told him: 'But I thought she was in for a simple procedure?'

'She is,' said the chap. 'But she's already complained about the food being cold, the sheets being threadbare, the toilet being dirty and the staff being unhelpful.'

ONE of the staff at a skin treatment clinic in Fraser's told us about treating a customer and asking her what her make-up removal routine was in the evening.

The lady simply replied: 'Pillow.'

AN elderly reader getting her prescription in Partick tells us the girl in front of her asked the assistant for a pregnancy testing kit. The assistant pointed to two or three different makes and asked which type she would like.

'A negative one, please,' the girl replied.

A READER swears he was in a Southside chemist's when a chap came in and asked the pharmacist if he had anything for hiccups.

Without warning, the pharmacist reached over and smacked the man between the shoulder blades and asked: 'Did that help?'

'I doubt it,' the customer replied. 'But if you like I'll go and check with my wife who is waiting out in the car.'

OUR occasional stories on National Service remind one older reader of reporting for his stint in uniform when he had to undertake a medical, and the doctor asked:

'Can you read the letters on the chart?'

'What letters?' replied our reader, hoping for a way out.

'Well,' replied the doctor, 'you've passed the hearing test.'

OUR favourite Western Infirmary story was when Celtic player Bobby Lennox was there after being stretchered off in an Old Firm game with a broken leg following a bruising tackle from Rangers captain John Greig. Propped up in the Western that evening with his leg in plaster Bobby was being interviewed for *Scotsport* when the reporter asked him when he realised his leg was broken.

'When I saw John Greig running towards me,' Bobby replied.

A CHAP in Mosspark tells us that he was trying to convince his ageing mother that a £900 hearing aid from a private company would be far better for her than the less helpful piece of equipment she had from the NHS, but she was having none of it. 'I've never heard a conversation yet,' she told him, 'that was worth £900.'

HOSPITALS can be confusing places. Reader Allison Gillespie in Glasgow was visiting her mum in hospital with her partner when the sweet old lady in the bed opposite shouted out: 'You're my daughter Mary!' Allison went over to calm her down and reassure her that she was not in fact her daughter. She thought it was all going well until she returned to her partner at her mum's bed only to hear the woman shout: 'Mary! That's not your husband, you slut!'

A GLASGOW pharmacist swears to us that a senior citizen came in for advice about a spot of constipation that had been troubling her. She said that for the past week, no matter how long she sat in the bathroom, nothing was happening.

'Did you take anything?' asked the pharmacist.

'Well, I took a magazine,' replied the puzzled lady.

A NURSE at Glasgow's old Southern General told us she was explaining to a recovering heart patient that his future health regime should include activity three times a week, which got his heart beating faster.

'Like shoplifting?' he asked.

A FIFE nurse swears to us that a patient recovering after an operation had to be told that he was going back into surgery as staff believed a swab had been left inside him and it had to be taken out.

'Here's ten pence,' said the patient. 'It cannae be worth more than that.'

A GLASGOW reader told us of a friend who had been called in for a check-up after registering with a different doctor following his move to a new address.

Said his pal: 'The doc said I should cut back on sugar in my diet, drink less alcohol and coffee, and reduce the stress in my life.

'So I said to him, "Fair enough. But realistically what should I do?"'

AN Ayrshire reader tells us a chap in his golf club was relating: 'Went to the doc's for my annual check-up. The practice nurse asked me to pop on the scales and, worried that I was going to get a lecture on putting on weight, I took off my boots, and then for good measure took my keys out of my pocket.

'"Do you want me to wait while you shave your eyebrows?" she asked me.'

COMMENTS a middle-aged woman: 'Pharmacist at the dispensary just asked if I was thirty-six, so I told him I'm actually forty-five but have a good skincare regime. Anyway, it turns out he was checking the address on the prescription and was referring to my house number not my age, so if you're looking for a prat I'll be over here.'

'I NEED that pint,' said the toper in the Glasgow pub at the weekend. 'I fell aff a fifteen-foot ladder this morning.' His pals quickly got him the pint before he added: 'I was only on the bottom rung. But still.'

To the person who stole my 4 year old grandaughters paddling pool, I hope you drown in it

OH my goodness, friends can be a bit sarky, can't they? A Glasgow reader was in town at the sales when she heard a young woman tell her pal:

'I'm thinking of buying a treadmill. Do you think they'll let me try it out first?'

'What are you going to do?' replied her pal. 'Ask them if you can bring your laundry in and hang damp clothes over it?'

WE remember the woman who recorded an increase in weight at her slimming club in Glasgow and, when asked what had caused it, said her hamster had died.

When she was asked if that had sparked off some comfort eating, she replied no, but she had been forced to finish a large box of Milk Tray as she needed the empty box to bury Whiskers.

AN Ayrshire reader tells us he was in his golf club bar when a younger player was talking enthusiastically about his fitness regime. As he left the bar, an older member further along commented: 'The last time I burned a thousand calories was when I forgot to keep an eye on the steak pie in the oven.'

GLASGOW is the second unhealthiest city in the UK, new research announced. It reminds us of a Glasgow reader who explained: 'You stand in the queue at Greggs admiring all the healthy salad options, low calorie juices, fruit, yoghurts, spring water, and when they shout "Next!" for some unexplainable reason you spurt forth with, "A steak bake, a packet ah cheese an' onion, an' a can ah Irn-Bru."'

AND a Glasgow reader once heard a young woman in a coffee shop queue tell her pal: 'I don't know whether I should have a cake as well.' And her pal replied: 'You're married now. You can eat whatever you want.'

A READER hears a classic misunderstanding in his canteen at work, where a young chap sits down and asks someone further down the table for the salt, which he then liberally pours over his dish.

The person passing the salt, possibly concerned about his health, asks the chap: 'Should you not taste it first?'

'Naw,' he replies. 'All salt tastes the same, doesn't it?'

'MY doc says I've to take up a hobby that gets me out of the pub,' said the toper in the pub the other night.

'So, I've taken up smoking,' he added.

TALES of protecting foodstuffs remind Ian Allingham: 'My dad was interned in Siam during the Second World War by the Japanese in a house which was serviced by a house boy.

'The internees noticed that the level of sherry in the decanter kept falling and one of them decided to replace half of the sherry with his own bodily fluid.

'This did not reduce the incidence of disappearing sherry so, after a few days, they confronted the house boy who explained that he was teetotal but did regularly use the sherry as an ingredient when cooking their evening meals.'

A DISCUSSION on smoking was taking place at an Ayrshire golf club when one chap declared to a smoker: 'So what is it now, eight quid a packet? At a packet a day that's nearly three grand a year. So over twenty years you could have bought an F-Type Jaguar.'

'Do you smoke?' the smoker replied.

'No,' said the chap.

'So where's your Jag?' asked the smoker.

MATERNITY stories remind a reader of the poster in the waiting room at the old Queen Mum's maternity hospital in Glasgow. He tells us: 'It read, "Have faith, the first few minutes of life are the most dangerous."'

'Someone had added the graffiti, "The last few are no' too clever either."'

TALKING of health, Andrew Foster, visiting from Canada, was on the train from Oban to Glasgow when two chaps were in a desperate hurry to get past the refreshment trolley in order to get to the toilet.

Says Andrew: 'After some shuffling and shunting the Glesga wummin in charge of the trolley managed to let them past, interrupting her sales patter just long enough to announce to everyone in the carriage, "Thae men – their prostates are a' gone!" and carried on selling coffee and sandwiches.

'I sat with my legs tightly crossed until we got to Glasgow.'

A PARTICK reader confesses to us that he is starting a diet right away after ordering a carry-out from his local Indian restaurant. When he unpacked the food he noticed the restaurant had included two sets of plastic cutlery rather than one.

PAISLEY reader Alan Barlow tells us: 'I was on the bus to the Royal Alexandra Hospital, and a couple of stops before the hospital a chap ran out of a shop clutching a roll and sausage and jumped on board.

'Nothing unusual about that except he was wearing pyjamas and slippers.

'As he disappeared into the hospital at journey's end two

things struck me – his resilience and the quality of hospital food.'

KEEPING fit is on many minds in January. 'I went out for a run at the weekend,' said a chap in a Glasgow bar to his pals. 'But had to go back after two minutes because I'd forgotten something.'

When a mate asked what, he added: 'I'd forgotten I'm fat, unfit and can't run for more than two minutes.'

AS others see us. A reader sends us a gag from an English webpage: 'Edinburgh man Wullie McTavish is on his death-bed, knows the end is near, is with the nurse, his wife, his daughter and two sons.

'"Bernie," he says. "I want you to take the Braid Hills houses. Sybil, take the flats over in Morningside and Bruntsfield. Tam, I want you to take the offices in Charlotte Square. Sarah, my dear wife, please take all the residential buildings in the New Town."

'The nurse is just blown away by all this and as Wullie slips away, she says, "Mrs McTavish, your husband must have been such a hard-working man to have accumulated all that property."

'"Property? The eedjit had a paper round."'

'THE bank phoned me because of suspicious activity on my credit card,' said the chap in the Glasgow pub the other night.

'They couldn't believe I'd joined a gym.'

A RETIRED Millport GP recalled being called out to see a young boy who became unwell on coming home from school. Examining the boy, the GP asked if he had passed water that day. The boy replied no, he hadn't, as he had come home by the back road.

16
Never Age

Growing old comes to us all of course, but we do like how *Herald* readers find the fun in it.

WE are told about the little boy visiting his granny who asked her, as his granddad had died many years ago, whether she was going to get a new boyfriend.

'This is my boyfriend now,' his granny told him, pointing to her old telly in the corner which was permanently on.

Imagine his parents' consternation, though, when he went home and casually mentioned: 'Granny was banging her boyfriend this afternoon.'

TALKING about ageing, a Pollokshields reader tells us: 'The computer constantly tells me to protect my password. I find at my age all my passwords are protected by amnesia.'

GROWING old, continued. Says David Donaldson: 'I have discovered that you can recreate the wonder and excitement of childhood simply by ordering a series of small items on the internet. Then, four or five days later, packages arrive at your door and you have not the faintest idea what it can be or who sent them. It's a bit like Christmas in the 1950s.'

SAYS a Pollokshaws reader: 'Surely I'm not the only person who religiously asks the wife on a Friday night what the plans are for the weekend and she tells me. Then on Saturday morning first thing I ask, "What are we doing this weekend?"'

A READER holidaying in America heard an elderly Scottish couple in front of him registering at a hotel. They were told their room had twin beds and asked if that was a problem.

'I don't know. We've been sharing the same bed for over thirty years,' the husband replied.

Our reader thought that was so romantic until the wife piped up: 'If he snores, how can I reach over and punch him when we're in separate beds?'

AIRDRIE stand-up Patrick Rolink said his grandfather had been a lifelong Airdrie supporter and, when he died, the family scattered his ashes over the pitch's centre circle.

'The ground was later sold and Safeways built a supermarket on it,' added Patrick. 'We do get some funny looks when we go back every year and leave flowers beside the fish counter.'

GERRY McCulloch tells us he suggested to his mother that she should write on the back of holiday photographs when and where they were taken.

Sometime later, when he was looking at them, he noticed she had written: 'Arran. Last week.'

WE can become a tad forgetful as we get older. A Milngavie pensioner parked his car in the car park behind the King's Theatre in Glasgow, and had to jump out to check he was within the parking bay. Anyway, after attending a play at the theatre for three hours, he couldn't find his car keys – he even got the assistant to check the row with her torch.

He then headed back to his car thinking he may have dropped the keys, and there they were in the ignition – with the engine still running.

A TOPER in a Glasgow pub was heard telling his drinking companions: 'I swear if my memory gets any worse I'll be able to plan my own surprise birthday party.'

AND a reader remarked: 'I thought I had a good memory until I get to the front of the queue and I'm asked what petrol pump I've just used.'

GLASGOW comedian Scott Agnew passes on: 'Old boy in Tesco to check-out assistant, "There'll be nae self-service for me, son – too bliddy complicated. And just you pack they bags fur us, cheers."

'He then steps back, produces a smartphone and skelps £20 away on his Skybet app.'

A WHITECRAIGS reader explains growing old to us: 'Childhood injuries: fell off my bike, fell out of a tree, twisted my ankle. Adult injuries: slept wrong, sat down too long, sneezed too hard.'

WHO can agree with Hannah Williams, who remarked on social media: 'I appreciate this marks my descent into a lonely death, surrounded by hundreds of cats, but I have now taken to picking up rubbish while walking around my neighbourhood...'

A friend replied: 'Keep us informed when you reach stage two, of shouting at random people in the park about minor infringement of council by-laws.'

A READER gets in touch with the news: 'According to a recent report, British men between fifty-five and sixty-five, will, on average, have sex two to three times per week. Japanese men in the same age group will have sex only once or twice per year.

'This has come as very upsetting news to most of my friends – they had no idea they were Japanese.'

A MOUNT FLORIDA reader confesses: 'In films it takes anyone who breaks into a car ten seconds to hot-wire it and drive away.

'Yet on holiday in Portugal last week it took me nearly fifteen minutes to find the switch that opened the flap over the petrol tank.'

'DOES the Queen ever study a freshly minted five pence

piece,' muses Tom Ferguson from Shettleston, 'then say to herself: "Ooft, I've let myself go?"'

MORE on growing old. Says Tim: 'Why is it I can somehow remember the lyrics of a song from the 1970s that I've probably not heard since then, yet I have to look at a boarding pass at least twenty times in quick succession to simply remember what seat I'm in?'

A SOUTHSIDE reader tells us: 'I was asked my age the other day in a shop and my mind suddenly went blank. So I thought I would quickly subtract the year of my birth from this year, but then for a moment I couldn't remember what year it is just now. So I just guessed how old I was.'

AN Ayr reader tells us about his elderly mother complaining that she kept missing parts of her television programmes when she went to put the kettle on or went to the toilet.

'You can get one of these digital boxes,' he told her. 'That freezes the programme while you are out of the room.'

'Naw, son, I couldn't do that,' she told him. 'It wouldn't be fair to all the other folk who were watching it.'

A READER tells us he was concerned about his ageing mum keeping a wad of banknotes in the top drawer of the bureau in the living room, which could be immediately spotted by any housebreaker.

As she refused to put the cash in the bank, he brought her instead a fake tin of beans which had a bottom, which could be removed for hiding cash inside and would not attract attention in the kitchen cupboard.

He was delighted on his next visit when she confirmed that she was using it – until he opened the bureau drawer in the living room, and there was the fake beans tin.

AN expatriate home from Cape Town was in a Dumfries post office when an elderly man at the front of the queue was being taken through some security questions in order to access his account. He was asked for his mother's maiden name. He said it was Mary. The man behind the counter explained that was her Christian name, not her maiden name.

As he stood there, looking blank, an exasperated voice shouted from the back of the queue: 'Mary whit?'

A MILNGAVIE reader liked the positive attitude of his ninety-year-old mother who broke a mirror and told him: 'Seven years' bad luck, which at my age can only be good news.'

THE perennial question of sex among senior citizens came up at a golf club, where a chap conceded he had sex with his wife about once a month.

Others concurred, but one bold pensioner said: 'With me, it's almost every night of the week.'

As his mates looked awestruck, he added: 'Monday, almost. Tuesday, almost. Wednesday . . .'

BAD weather brings out the caring side in us. Alistair Magill passed an elderly couple tottering into East Kilbride shopping centre yesterday.

'I was impressed,' he said, 'to see the husband taking his wife's arm in his, as the ground was slippery with the new snow.

'Only when I got closer did I hear him say nice and clearly, "Now if you fall, let go of me, as you're no taking me wi' ye."

'Chivalry and wedded bliss.'

A GRANDFATHER visiting his family in Newton Mearns at the weekend watched as his grandson put on elbow pads, knee pads and a helmet before announcing: 'I'm going to ride my bike, Grand-da.'

'Where?' asked the puzzled old fella. 'Through a minefield?'

RETIREMENT can mean quite a life change for many people. A senior citizen from the Southside of Glasgow tells us the talk at the bowling club the other day was what time did retirees go to bed, now that they no longer had to get up for their work in the morning.

One chap explained his regime by telling them: 'My bedtime is three hours after I fall asleep on the couch.'

ONE third of men in a survey admitted to having a midlife crisis, with many splashing out on sports cars or motorbikes.

A reader attended the fiftieth birthday party of a friend, who had treated himself to a large, fast motorbike, where another pal told the birthday boy: 'We clubbed together to get you what we thought would be the most appropriate gift,' and handed him an organ donor card.

GROWING old continued. A reader in Jordanhill tells us: 'It really is hard to convey to young people the excitement we all genuinely felt at school when the teacher wheeled in an overhead projector to the classroom.'

A READER getting the bus into Glasgow was much taken with a couple of pensioners behind him discussing a mutual friend. 'She saw a pair of shoes she fancied in the charity shop, but said they were too dear.'

'Too dear in a charity shop?' replied her pal. 'What's she going to do, then? Rummage through bins?'

WE mentioned growing concerns about elderly drivers, and a Dunblane reader tells us about his father-in-law who got lost between Ayr and Dunblane, and ended up in Bishop-briggs, eventually arriving home hours late.

When his family questioned him on how he ended up in Bishopbriggs, he blamed the taxi he was following.

'But why did you follow the taxi?' asked his family.

'Because I reckoned he would know where he was going,' came the indignant reply.

MORE on forgetfulness with Bill Garven telling us he was in a car park beside his Honda Civic when he pressed the remote control on his key and a car at the other end of the car park beeped its horn and flashed its lights in response.

Says Bill: 'Striding purposefully towards the other car, already making up my letter of complaint to Honda and simply to take a note of the car registration number, imagine my surprise to discover it had the same registration plate as my own.'

A READER confesses: 'I was telling a story involving a bus conductor. My son asked, "What is a bus conductor?" When I explain, my daughter says she thought I had said "a busking doctor".'

17
Technology Fails

It may frustrate and bamboozle us at times, but we can still get a laugh when faced with ever-changing technology.

A READER in Hyndland emails us with some safety advice: 'You should never text while you are driving. All it takes is one moment of distraction and suddenly everyone in the group chat thinks you can't spell.'

AN Edinburgh reader tells us: 'I went into a café the other day and there was a sign on the counter which said, "We have no wi-fi. Pretend it's like the old days."

'So I gave them forty pence for my coffee and lit up a fag. Apparently that's not what they meant.'

'I WENT round to visit my father who has retired,' says a Bearsden reader, 'and he showed me his new mobile phone which he has in a protective case that looks strong enough to survive being run over.

'But all I could think about was us growing up as children when Dad was driving the family car and he didn't even bother to tell us to put on seat belts.'

YES, many parents happily now text their children, which is not always appreciated. One Glasgow teenager showed us a text from his mother in reply to one of his which contained the usual abbreviations. Texted his mother: 'It's before, not b4. I speak English, not bingo.'

DO we believe the reader who tells us: 'My wife told me the butter in the fridge was rock hard, and could I help spread it.

So I went on to Facebook and told everyone that our butter was rock hard.

'Apparently that's not what she meant.'

'I'M getting old,' a *Herald* reader remarked to his teenage daughters the other day. 'When I was young I managed to go for months without taking a picture of anything.'

LISTENING to music has changed so much in recent years, what with folk listening to tracks on shuffle on their iPods or mobile phones.

As one reader told us: 'My friends were discussing when they had last listened to an album in its entirety. One of them replied, "The last time TalkTalk put me on hold."'

TALKING of social media, we pass on the message posted by American TV station NBC News which stated: 'Isis fighters are shaving bears and hiding in civilian homes to avoid air strikes.'

Two minutes later it added: 'Correction: it was beards, not bears.'

A YOUNG woman revealed on a Facebook page for citizens of Glasgow's Dennistoun that: 'This morning I went to fetch my washing off the line and all my underwear was gone. Feeling a little creeped out.'

Fellow Dennistonians expressed their disgust at such a

theft, although one chap did reply: 'My neighbour once came to my door asking if I'd stolen her underwear from the washing line. I nearly wet her pants!'

THE stress of being a teenager. A reader heard his daughter look up from her mobile phone and state: 'Some people have written "Happy Birthday" on my timeline without any exclamation marks. It's as if they don't even care.'

MANY folk now have an Amazon Echo in their homes. A Glasgow reader swears he asked, while hosting a Boxing Day party that was going on too long: 'Alexa, send everyone home.' He claims the electronic device then played a Sydney Devine recording.

A GLASGOW reader reports a dilemma which many of us face these days. She says: 'I wake up saying to myself that I have so much to do and worry that there are not enough hours in the day. A couple of hours later I'm somehow doing a quiz on Facebook to discover what my gangster name would be.'

WE liked the comment from a young woman named Chloe who passes on:

'Still canny get over the fact a boy at work said "Y for young team" to a customer when he was spelling something out using the phonetic alphabet.'

PROBLEMS that new technology brings with it. Says James Hinton: 'The fingerprint scanner on my smartphone doesn't work if your finger is too warm, too cold, pressed down lightly or pressed down too hard. It's the Goldilocks of phones.'

A NEWS story stating that using mobile phones after ten p.m. can trigger depression and loneliness reminded a reader:

'I used to take my mobile phone to bed but stopped after I dropped it one night and thought it had bounced under the bed. I got down on my knees, peered under the bed and couldn't see it.

'Without thinking, I noticed my phone lying beside my leg so I picked it up and used the light in the phone to look for it under the bed. Then the penny dropped.'

18

Man's Best Friend

We all love pets surely. And they can often bring a smile to our lips.

A CHAP taking an early-morning constitutional through his local cemetery saw a fellow walker, and shouted out a cheery, 'Morning!'

But the fellow he saw shouted back: 'No. Just walking my dog.'

A WORKER in a Paisley factory recalled a colleague who told everyone of the drama of his chip pan going on fire the previous night and the fire brigade being called out to save their house.

He had reached the point in his tale where he said that the family dog had gone for the fireman when an astonished listener, presumably brought up on too many *Lassie* films, asked: 'Your dog ran all the way to the fire station?'

'Naw,' explained the chap. 'He went for the first fireman through the door and sank his teeth into him.'

DOG owners will no doubt agree with Liz Hackett who points out: 'Having an older dog means ten seconds after you drop a piece of food, you have to drop an even bigger piece of food so they can find it.'

FORMER Celtic and St Mirren star Frank McAvennie, at the launch of old St Mirren mate Billy Abercromby's auto-biography, told of the time Aber turned up at a club night out in Glasgow wearing a sheepskin jacket and slippers.

Said Frank: 'When we asked Billy why he was wearing slippers, he told us he had been walking his dog and had suddenly remembered about the night out. He then legged it straight from his dog-walking to the nightclub. When we asked where the dog was, Billy said he just put it on a bus going in the opposite direction and asked the driver to let it off at the next stop.'

NEWS from Australia where the state of New South Wales has banned greyhound racing after claims of cruelty. It reminds us of a reader who has a retired greyhound as a pet who can't resist it when people stop him in the park and ask:
   'Did you ever race it?'
   Replying: 'No, not fit enough at my age.'

A PIECE of whimsy from Jake Lambert who says: 'Imagine if dogs worked out that they are actually full of bones.'

A READER tells us she brought home a kitten for the family, even though her husband didn't seem too keen.
   As he sat reading his newspaper, she was flicking a piece of paper on the floor for the kitten to chase and then happily declared: 'We should get him a ball of wool.'
   'What, can he knit as well?' came the bored voice from behind the paper.

CLIMATE change was being discussed in a Motherwell pub the other day where a regular opined: 'They say that if the planet keeps on warming up, the only place where you will be able to see a polar bear is in a zoo.'
   'So,' he added, 'no change there for us then.'

WE are told about a distraught dog owner who took her pet to the vet because of an unusual growth in the poor mutt's mouth.

After examining it, the vet asked the owner if she had any children. 'Oh, my God! Is it contagious?' she shouted.

'No,' the bemused vet replied. 'It's bubble gum.'

A READER buying his car insurance on a popular online site noted a message popped up asking: 'Would you also like a quote to insure your pet?'

He said to himself: 'Surely no one lets their dog drive the car.'

FORMER rugby star Doddie Weir, whose autobiography *My Name'5 Doddie* is now a bestseller, was speaking in Galashiels about the book which details his career and coping with Motor Neuron Disease. Doddie, who helps on the family farm nearby, took questions from the audience, and after the first two questions about Borders rugby rivalry and playing for the Lions, he then realised how special the Borders can be. The third question was from a local who asked: 'Why did you no' buy any sheep from me this year?'

WE doubt very much that someone went into a pet shop to buy a goldfish and when the assistant asked: 'Do you want an aquarium?'

Replied: 'I really don't care what star sign it is.'

ON a rare sunny day, a Glasgow chap was telling his mates in the pub that there had been a couple of wasps in his house and he took it upon himself to get out the fly spray.

'It said on the can,' he told them, 'not to spray near the eyes. But how can you be that accurate with a flying insect? So I just thought, to hang with that, and sprayed the whole wasp.'

THERE is the daft joke of the minister who lost his Bible when out for a walk, then couldn't find it. He prayed for its safe return and, two days later, a dog came to his door with the Bible in its mouth.

'It's a miracle!' shouted the delighted minister.

'Not really,' replied the dog. 'Your name was written inside the cover.'

READER Donald Macdonald tells us about the uniquely Glaswegian words of encouragement as the cyclists on the Pedal for Scotland charity run from Glasgow to Edinburgh were going through Easterhouse. One chap with a large Alsatian shouted: 'If youse get tired oan the next hill, I'll let him aff his lead.'

A CHAP in Newton Mearns had obviously taken his brave pills when he went with his wife to a cat rescue centre to choose a family pet. After picking up a variety of cats of all different shapes and colours, she held two in her arms, and asked him which he preferred.

'The striped one makes you look thinner,' he couldn't help himself saying.

FORMER Clyde Valley Stompers musician Peter Kerr, who wrote a series of books about living in Majorca, told us that, on their first Christmas there, the old Majorcan farmer across the road offered to sweep their clogged chimney.

Said Peter: 'He arrived with a ladder and a sack containing his chimney-sweeping apparatus, then emptied the contents of the sack down the chimney.

'There was much noise from up the lum, heaps of soot came tumbling down, followed by the "apparatus" – a live hen. It worked a treat. The hen just shook off the soot, clucked indignantly and wandered back over the lane.'

A WHIMSICAL reader phones to tell us: 'Just said "boo" to a goose. Don't see what all the fuss is about.'

IT'S great to have a dog on long summer nights. Many an owner will agree with Amy Vansant who tells us: 'I swear that my dog spends half his time trying to understand what we're saying to him, and the other half trying to pretend he doesn't understand what we're saying to him.'

THE news that the Scottish Government has banned wild animals in travelling circuses reminds us of the teacher who was explaining to her colleagues that she had been to a circus where an elephant was made to wear a skirt while performing.

'It was a right shame,' said the teacher. 'The poor thing was peeing all the time.'

'Was it incontinent?' asked an anxious colleague.

'No, it was in Stranraer,' came the reply.

HAVE you ever seen one of those little round robot vacuum cleaners that you leave to wander by itself around a room? Kenneth Gosnold tells us about his: 'My dog doesn't like the robot vacuum, and proceeds to bark at it. Today, though, the vacuum presented the dog with an empty Coke bottle it found under the coffee table. The dog and the robot vacuum are now best friends, with the dog dutifully following it around the house hoping it finds more treats for him.'

A READER sends us a message put on social media: 'A mate overslept and had to get on a flight within an hour, so he shoved all the clothes on his bed into his suitcase. When he got to the airport he found out he'd packed his cat.'

AN Edinburgh reader phones about the news that Edinburgh Zoo pandas Tian Tian and Yang Guang have failed to mate, and tells us:

'It's Edinburgh. Someone needed to explain to him that he should have bragged about his property portfolio and bought her buckets of Champagne first. Then it wouldn't have been a problem.'

SCOTTISH ex-pat Kate Woods recalls moving to the out-skirts of New Orleans some years ago and looking out of the window to see a goat grazing in the garden.

Says Kate: 'I chased it away before it could do any more damage to my flower beds. A short while later a neighbour rang the doorbell and said, "I know that you come from a foreign country so I thought that I should let you know that the animal in your yard this morning is called a goat and is relatively harmless."

'I thanked him kindly.'

19
Bit of a Dish

Even the government realised how important eating out can be by subsidising cheap deals during the summer. Here are some of the happier tales of dining out.

A SCOTTISH seaman ordered a giant lobster claw in a Rio de Janeiro restaurant.

Unfortunately the claw was in a scabby condition, badly cracked and chipped. When he complained, the waiter told him it was due to the lobsters fighting in the tanks.

'Well,' said the Scot, 'take this one back tae the kitchen and bring us oot the winner.'

A LADY having lunch in Glasgow was not impressed by her tired-looking chocolate cake. She sniffed it and declared: 'It smells like cocoa.'

The smug waiter told her: 'It's chocolate cake. It should smell like cocoa.'

'Coco's my dog,' she replied.

'I DON'T gossip myself,' confided the woman in a Glasgow coffee shop to her friend. 'But I do like to pass on snippets to people who do,' she added.

MIKE Ritchie was in a hotel, which is now closed funnily enough, in Angus, where an American diner complained that his steak was tough and the vegetables undercooked.

'Nothing like speaking your mind is there, sir?' said the waiter, before walking away.

WE do wonder how foreigners cope with Scotland at times. A Kilmarnock reader was having lunch in a local restaurant when his wife asked for cream with her sticky toffee pudding.

'Pouring or skooshy?' asked the waitress.

BARBECUES have meant a few chaps having to meet their neighbours for the first time socially. We are told of one such gathering in Bishopbriggs, where a chap collecting his burger asked a neighbour he didn't know:

'So what do you do?'

'Oh, I've got a finger in a few pies,' the neighbour bumptiously declared.

'So you're banned from Greggs then?' our burger-eater replied before his wife dragged him away.

HAVE you noticed some restaurant menus are becoming more Americanised these days? A reader was in one such restaurant where the menu stated your steak came with a choice of a side dish. This escaped the notice of the chap at the next table who was asked how he would like his steak cooked.

After he replied: 'Medium,' the waitress asked: 'And which side?'

After a certain hesitation, the chap replied: 'Both.'

A PARTICK reader is feeling a bit down in the dumps after his family took him out to a West End restaurant to celebrate his forty-fifth birthday. His wife sneaked a birthday cake to the staff for them to bring out after the meal and handed the waitress two candles shaped as '4' and a '5' to put on it.

Our reader is crushed that the young waitress looked over at him and then asked his wife what order the two numbers should go on the cake.

WE hear a woman in a Renfield Street bar confess to her pals: 'Was in by myself on Saturday and ordered a pizza from Domino's. It was so big that I shouted, "Pizza's here!" into an empty room so the delivery boy wouldn't judge me.'

A MOTHER tells us she got 'a bit of a reddy' when she took her young children to a family reunion in a restaurant and ordered a bottle of wine for the company. When the waiter brought the bottle and poured a little into her glass to taste, the moment was spoiled by her nine-year-old loudly remarking: 'Mummy usually has a lot more than that.'

A LATE-NIGHT reveller in Glasgow couldn't fault the logic of the young girl serving in the chip shop when he asked for a bag of chips and she inquired if he wanted regular or large.

Not sure of the quantities involved, he asked what the difference was.

'You get mair chips,' she replied.

A COLLEAGUE was telling a Glasgow reader of his trip with the family to a fast food restaurant where there were so many dishes from the previous occupants on the table that he spent the first five minutes clearing them up.

'Did the staff say thanks?' asked our reader.

'Thank me?' the chap replied. 'My picture's up on the wall as employee of the month.'

WHEN there was the scandal of horsemeat being used in meat dishes at a supermarket, a young waitress at a Glasgow burger joint pleaded with her customers to come up with some new patter. She said that whenever she asked if they wanted anything on their burger, she wants them to know they were not the first to tell her: 'Five pounds each way.'

AN Edinburgh reader noticed a city chip shop that had to display a notice in its window from health inspectors detailing an infestation of mice discovered on the premises. No doubt the notice was ordered by health inspectors as a deterrent. But our reader wonders how effective it was.

Someone else had taped a notice to the outside of the window on which they had written: 'Who cares about mice? I dinnae go tae a chippy tae get healthy.'

TALES of army catering remind a Kelvinside reader of lining up for food in the mess where the cooked food looked so vile he put only a piece of cake on his tray. The cook asked him if that was all he was having, and when he replied that the rest didn't look very appetising, the cook asked in that case if he would like two slices of cake.

When our reader replied in the affirmative, the cook leaned across and cut the cake on his tray in half.

RAGTIME blues band Pokey LaFarge & the South City Three, asked in a radio interview what they were doing after their show, said they would be cooking a 'four-pint chicken dish' which their manager from Paisley had shown them. When asked for the recipe, St Louis-born Pokey replied: 'You throw the chicken in the pan with some potatoes, carrots, onions and stock. Then go out to the pub for four pints. When you return, it's ready.'

CHRISTMAS nights out at hotels, and Barry McGirr at the Leapark Hotel in Grangemouth told us: 'We've comedian Gary Skyner appearing at our Christmas Dinner Shows.

'He was telling the partygoers the other night that he'd been tending his wife's grave in the morning.

'"She's not aware of that of course," he said. "She thinks it's a fishpond."'

20
Courting Attention

Even an encounter with our courts and meeting the constabulary can be turned into a joke by our readers.

INDEFATIGABLE advocate Donald Findlay once told of a client who had thrown a petrol bomb into a Govan pub. 'Fortunately,' said Donald, 'someone drank it before it went off.'

RETIRED Scottish football referee Willie Young also has a successful career as a lawyer, which is why he was saying he had to tell a client held in jail that there was good news and bad news about the analysis of some blood found at the scene of the crime.

The bad news, said Willie, was that the blood was a match for his.

'So what's the good news?' asked the client.

'Your cholesterol level is right down,' said Willie.

A GLASGOW lawyer swears to us that he was in the sheriff court one day when the accused, giving evidence in his defence, claimed he was not there at the time of the alleged offence as he had 'shot the craw'.

The sheriff bestirred himself at this point, shuffled his papers and declared: 'I didn't know there were guns involved.'

A READER once claimed that he was in a pub in Glasgow's East End where the discussion turned to TV celebrities, and a local chipped in with: 'I was on the telly once.'

Then added: 'Well, not me exactly, but an artist's sketch of me.'

BROADCASTER Dougie Donnelly, presenting the Law Awards of Scotland at Glasgow's Hilton Hotel, recalled that he himself achieved a law degree at Strathclyde University before working in radio.

'I was telling the wife,' he reminisced, 'that when I was at Strathclyde studying law, never in my wildest dreams did I imagine that I would one day present the Scottish law awards.

'She told me that, funnily enough, I was never in her wildest dreams either.'

WE hear the folk in Airdrie were in a state of shock over the news that guns used in a gangland killing were found dumped behind a library in neighbouring Coatbridge last week.

They had no idea that Coatbridge had a library.

A GLASGOW reader tells us of recently doing her bit as a jury member. When she and her fourteen colleagues entered the jury room, a fellow jurist piped up:

'He looks so smart. I don't think he would so such a thing.'

A fellow member quickly pointed out to her that they had merely gone into the room to store their coats, and it was normal to wait until after they had heard the evidence before taking a decision.

WE mentioned the death of Glasgow Sheriff J. Irvine Smith, and a lawyer passes on:

'He was trying a drink-driving case where the accused has been aggressive and offensive with the traffic polis. Found guilty, the accused launches into a long monologue, begging not to be disqualified.

'When he finishes, Irvine looks gravely at him over his half-moons and says, "Go and take a f*** to yersel" and "This is just a load of s****!"

'Stunned silence in courtroom, many thinking the learned sheriff has finally lost it, only for him to continue, "That's what you said to the officers when they asked you to give a breath test. I can find no room for special reasons."'

IT'S great the way the police are using social media to contact people. Yorkshire Police in Kirklees posted a picture of a wedding couple and asked:

'Do you recognise this couple? A wedding album featuring them was found dumped in a bin in Holmforth and we'd like to give it back.'

Only an hour later the police then added: 'Mystery solved. Looks like the album was handed in to us in good faith, but the owner doesn't want it back.'

BIG problem in Scottish prisons is hidden mobile phones. A prison officer tells us they received a phone call from a mother asking if they could pass on a message to her son that she had put £20 credit on his phone. The officer asked for the phone's number which she innocently rattled off. The officer then walked to the prisoner's cell, took out his own phone and dialled the number. At 'hello', he opened the door, met the gaze of the bemused felon, then duly confiscated the illicit device.

A GLASGOW lawyer tells us of a colleague representing a client in a divorce case and how he had asked her to write down her income and outgoings. At the end where she wrote what she had left over every month she had simply put 'F.A.'

When he stood up and told the sheriff that she had absolutely no income left when the bills were paid his client looked confused and whispered to him: 'Family allowance.'

'WAS interviewed by the police, but just said "No comment" to every question,' said the young lad in the pub. 'Thinking back, that's probably why I didn't get the job.'

A RECENTLY retired lawyer phones to tell us: 'I still think back to the first trial I took as a young solicitor and after winning I rushed back to the office, charged in and declared loudly, "Justice prevailed!"

'My boss, without even looking up, replied: "Ah well, we can always think about an appeal."'

READER Sandy Tuckerman passes on the story from musician Phil Cunningham about when his sports car was set on fire by thieves many years ago in their frustration at not being able to get it started.

Says Sandy: 'The police arrived promptly and while they surveyed the smouldering wreck in Edinburgh's Gorgie one of the officers asked him what make it was. Phil told him it was an MGB GT. To ensure his notes were accurate the constable asked, "Could you spell that, please?"'

THE scene was a Glasgow court, where the accused vehemently denied a charge of shoplifting. The problem, as is often the case, was that the prosecution had a videotape showing quite clearly the accused in the act of purloining the goods in question.

The accused watched the video which, incontrovertibly, showed footage of him stuffing items up his jook. He appeared despondent. Suddenly he cheered up considerably and even leaped to his feet in elation. 'Look,' he cried. 'I put the stuff back.'

'Naw, son. We're just rewinding the tape,' said the court officer.

JAMES Fraser tells us about a report filed in the old Partick police office in Glasgow by a probationer who stated that a house fire had been caused by an electrical fitting falling from the ceiling and igniting the carpet below.

A more senior officer reading the report thought this sounded so unusual that he phoned the fire station to check. Much laughter at the police station when the firefighter looked at his records and explained that the fire had been caused by a dropped light.

AN Edinburgh reader tells us he attended a business dinner where a chap at his table, after a few libations, launched into a lengthy tale about suing a company, but the case got tied up in the courts. Our reader thought it was going to be awkward when the chap ended his story belligerently with: 'In the end, the only people who got any money were the bloody lawyers!' as there were a couple of lawyers at the table.

He didn't have to worry as one of the lawyers filled the ensuing silence by opining: 'Oh, I do like a story with a happy ending.'

A RETIRED police officer tells us they arrested a young chap for car theft, but as he appeared to be under the influence of drink or drugs they asked the police doctor to have a look at him.

In the cell the doctor gave the confused chap a shake and asked him: 'I'm a doctor. Did you take anything?'

The befuddled chap replied: 'A Peugeot 207.'

'I WAS stopped by a traffic cop,' said the loudmouth in the pub. 'He came up and asked me, "Do you know why I stopped you, sir?"

'So I told him, "Well if you can't remember, I'm not going to remind you."'

A FORMER Strathclyde traffic officer tells us of the cheekiest motorist he ever stopped. After flagging down a driver who went through a red light, the police officer asked him: 'Didn't you see the red light?'

'The light, yes,' the driver replied. 'But you? No.'

THE scaffolding had come down from the Britannia Panopticon on Glasgow's Argyle Street after sandstone cleaning.

Irene Graham, chair of the Panopticon Trust, which is preserving one of the oldest music halls in the world, is delighted not only that its removal means people can see the building in all its glory, but it also stops sneak thieves who have been using the scaffolding to break into the auditorium.

She tells us: 'One cheeky thief thought he'd fool the local

constabulary by posing as a dummy alongside the Victoriana-clad mannequins which are dotted about the balcony and auditorium.

'Sadly for him, his tracksuit and trainers gave him away.'

REPORTER Alan Fisher, now with the Al Jazeera news network, was once covering the High Court in Aberdeen for Northsound Radio when a witness was asked if she saw the person responsible for the crime.

Says Alan: 'My heart sank as she pointed in my direction with the classic, "Aye there he is there."'

'It was enough to cause a small uproar in the court. Just as things were dying down, it erupted again when one of the five accused turned round and said, "We were wi' him."'

FORMER Justice Minister Kenny MacAskill was in Dundee's Whitfield estate making a speech on recovering goods from criminal gangs. A police officer tells us about the time his police football team was playing in Whitfield, one of the more challenging housing schemes and, having been told there had been robberies from the changing rooms, decided to keep all their valuables locked in their van when they played. The van was nicked.

A READER tells us about the Glasgow defendant, pleading guilty to slashing someone in a street affray, whose lawyer was overcome with verbosity and told the sheriff:

'My client realises that the Sword of Damocles is hanging over him but I would ask for leniency.'

The sheriff merely replied: 'It's not the Sword of Damocles that concerns me in this case but the Knife of Stanley.'

GLASGOW Airport terror attack icon, cigarette-smoking baggage handler John Smeaton, is appearing at the Edinburgh Fringe in *An Audience with John Smeaton*. At a preview show in Glasgow, John explained his philosophy that if he saw a polis being attacked, he would go and help him.

The point was perhaps spoiled by an audience member interrupting: 'I'm frae the Gallowgate and if I see a polisman being attacked, I'd be right in there giving him a kicking, too.'

Incidentally, John explained why he was having a fag outside the airport at the time of the attack: he was calming his nerves before having to tell his supervisor that he hadn't loaded golf clubs in time for the Malaga flight which had gone off with the golfers on board.

WE remember the chap in Bearsden building an extension, who was approached by a chap offering to sell him suspiciously cheap bricks.

Not wishing to overlook a bargain, he agreed – only to discover the brick seller had taken the bricks already stacked in the back of his garden and delivered them to the front.

When he went to the police, they warned him that if they

were to arrest the thief, they would have to arrest him as well for buying stolen goods.

WE are sent a newspaper cutting of a Glasgow court case where a woman, attacked by an ex-boyfriend, is giving evidence, and the fiscal, to show the woman seldom went out, asked her: 'So this was a rare night out?'

'Hardly a rare night out. I got stabbed,' the woman replied.

RANDOM Edinburgh Fringe gag: 'I wish I hadn't arrested a magician last night,' said the policeman. 'The trouble started when I asked him to empty his pockets.'

IT'S tough being a lawyer these days, or so they tell us. A Glasgow lawyer was bemoaning the fact the downturn in the housing market had affected the once lucrative conveyancing business, and that much of his turnover was now coming from dealing with wills and estates. 'Mind you,' he added, 'this mild winter hasn't helped with that either.'

EVEN when confronted by the law, Glaswegians feel the need to make a joke. Former detective Gerard Gallacher tells in his autobiography *Gangsters, Killers and Me* of accompanying Belgian detectives to Balornock to confront a thief accused of robbing stores in their country.

A Belgian officer asked the accused in quaint English: 'Are you a member of a club of international cash register thieves?'

The Balornock chap merely replied: 'No, I am no longer a member of that particular club. I let my membership lapse as the renewal fees were far too high.'

A MILNGAVIE reader on the bus into Glasgow realised that some folk live in a different world from him when he heard a young chap tell his pal on the bus: 'Ma phone was dead for two days as I'd lost the charger.

'Everyone thought I was in the jail.'

A GLASGOW lawyer tells us he had an elderly couple in his office this week making wills for the first time.

On reflection, he tells us, he wished he hadn't said to them: 'Which one of you wants to go first?'

A GLASGOW lawyer swears on oath to us that a recidivist appearing at a Justice of the Peace Court for some drink-related crime was told by the exasperated JP that the accused had been appearing before him for the past ten years.

The accused merely replied: 'It's not my fault you can't get promoted.'

TONY Sykes in Glasgow was in court when a young man who had been charged with being drunk and incapable in the nurses' hostel at the local hospital asked if he could call the nurses as witnesses to confirm he had not been incapable, as 'ah've ma' reputation to think of,' as he explained.

OUR tales of courts dealing with drunken offenders remind retired police officer Colin Simpson of the inspector at Glasgow's Govan police office who, when drunks kept in the cell overnight were brought before him to be bailed in the morning, would simply ask them in mock surprise: 'How did you end up in Rothesay?' before sending the worried lags out into the streets of Govan.

ANDREW Stalker tells us about Falkirk police using a sniffer dog at club queues to detect drugs. When the dog stopped next to a group and barked, a girl broke down, confessing she was under eighteen, but how could the dog possibly know? It turned out it had detected drugs on a chap behind her, and was not, as she'd thought, trained to work out folk's ages.

RETIRED police inspector turned crime novelist Les Brown told us that, many years ago in the Gorbals, police recruits were taken on the beat and led into the cellar of the vast Co-op headquarters in Morrison Street where the coffins were stored.

Says Les: 'After a few minutes the lid of a coffin would slide sideways and a shrouded figure, which was of course another cop, sat up.

'The practice came to a sudden end when a young cop struck the shrouded figure with his baton before exiting the building.'

A BBC film about Scotland's famous safe-cracker Gentle Johnny Ramensky, reminded retired reporter Gordon Airs of interviewing another safe-blower, Paddy Meehan, who told him that he did a bank job with Johnny towards the end of his criminal career.

Searching about in the dark for the safe, Johnny whispered that he had found it.

Recalled Paddy: 'I padded up and saw it was a fridge. I opened the door and the light came on. He said his eyes weren't what they used to be, and I said, "You're no' kidding."

'When we found the safe I let him put on the plastic explosive. He was always so finicky – he just wanted the door to swing open perfectly. I packed in a lot more and he complained that it would blow the door off. I said: "Listen, it's no' oor safe."'

A PARTICK reader was amongst a large crowd on Dumbarton Road held back because of the police siege on the flat where a chap had barricaded himself in.

She tells us: 'Two old dears pushed to the front and asked what was going on.

'"The polis are watching that," a chap replied. "The guy's keepin' a hostage up there."

'"Hear that, Mary," said the woman to her pal. "The police are here with their guns 'cause somebody's keeping horses in his flat."'

GOING home from the city centre, a reader witnessed two police officers warning a rowdy drunk that he'd be locked up for the night if he didn't behave.

'What's the charge?' shouted the aggressive drunk.

It went over his head when one officer replied: 'Oh there's no charge. It's a free service.'

OUR mention of the robust dancing at the Highlanders' Institute in Glasgow reminded Paul O'Sullivan: 'My parents used to go to a ceildih there on a Saturday evening. At that time dances had to finish before midnight on a Saturday to avoid people having fun on the Sabbath.

'Every Saturday half a dozen big Heilin' cops used to turn up at the ceilidh about 11.30 p.m.

'They would check out the dance and all the conditions very seriously, then they would take off their caps and dance reels till five to midnight when they would put their caps back on and tell the band to stop playing.'

POLICE forces are now using social media to connect with the public. Police in Falkirk had a go by putting on Twitter:

'A wall in Kinneil Drive, Bo'ness was damaged at weekend. Black spray paint used to graffiti it. Words "MOLLY" and "FIONA". Who did this?'

Inevitably someone replied: 'Just a hunch. But you should maybe concentrate on looking for two women called Molly and Fiona.'

COMEDY writer Phil Differ's show about prison life, *Who's Afraid of the Big Bar-L*, was previewed at Barlinnie Prison, where the prisoners chatted to the performers afterwards.

One prisoner interested in the production was asked if he himself had tried acting.

'Yes,' he replied. 'At Glasgow Sheriff Court. I wasn't very good.'

21

Burning Books

Some stories just cannot be categorised, so here is a very wonderful mixture.

WE asked for your library stories, and Sylvia Russell in Lanark recounts: 'I returned a tattered library book and, rather embarrassed, explained that our puppy had chewed it up, and so offered to pay for it. I remarked that they must hear a lot of strange excuses, and the librarian said that a woman who came in to pay for a lost book said she had used it to prop up the head of her recently departed husband for an open coffin viewing, and had forgotten to remove it before he was cremated.'

WE pass on this observation from writer Sanjeev Kohli, who confirms something we've long suspected.

Says Sanjeev: 'The main reason for bottle banks is to give middle-class people some idea of what a fight sounds like.'

A BEARSDEN reader is still thinking about the observation he heard a young woman make on the train into Glasgow the other day. She looked at the back of her hand then told her pal: 'Just imagine how much time you would save over the year if we were born with red nails.'

AT Halloween a Newton Mearns reader told us she had prepared little plastic pumpkins filled with sweets and fruit to hand out to the kids who came to the door. All the children took them and said thank you, apart from one little tot who raked through the pumpkin, pulled out a tangerine, handed it back to our reader and said: 'I'll not be needing this.'

A COLLEAGUE comes over to tell us: 'My parents said that if I was to get a tattoo I should get it done in a place that doesn't really matter and is out of sight.

'So I had it done in Bellshill.'

WE asked about removals, and Eunan Coll tells us:

'A friend in Glasgow's Southside was pottering about in his front garden when he spotted a large removal lorry outside the house four doors down. There was a woman issuing instructions to the driver and when the lorry moved off my friend toddled along, stuck out his hand and said:

[281]

"'Welcome to the Avenue. I hope you will be happy here, and if you have any problems I live just four doors along."

"'Thanks very much,' she replied, 'but my family are just leaving – we've been living here for the past eleven years.'"

A WEST END reader told us her church took the children to a homeless centre in Glasgow to entertain the residents. As they trooped into the centre, one worthy standing outside drawing on a roll-up asked: 'Whit's goin' on in there the night, hen?'

Our reader told him: 'The children from our church are doing their nativity play.'

He took a further drag before asking: 'Oh, aye. Whit's it aboot?'

A BEARSDEN reader tells us her seventeen-year-old daughter is learning to drive and offered to take her parents to church on Sunday. When they arrived the teenage girl's dad said: 'Thank you.'

When their daughter said he didn't have to thank her, he replied: 'I was talking to God.'

A PIECE of daftness from Gary Delaney who says: 'I was staying at a friend's who said, "I'll make up the spare room for you." He was true to his word. He didn't have a spare room.'

COPYING other people's speeches came up, and Ian Young told us:

'As an inveterate note-taker myself, when attending dinners, of other speakers' jokes for my own later use, I have long been aware of the possible admonition from the top table speaker of "Am I speaking slowly enough for you to take them down?"

'To deal with this I have developed a ready response of, "Oh I'm not writing them down, I'm ticking them off."'

A READER confessed to her pal that she had a panic room. Her bemused pal replied: 'What? One of those secure rooms rich people go into if they think they are under attack?'

'No' she replied, 'A panic room where you throw in all the clutter quickly when someone arrives at your house unexpectedly.'

WITH Easter approaching, a bar-room philosopher declared the other night: 'Let's be honest, if it wasn't for Easter eggs and Christmas presents, Christianity would be long gone by now.'

'I DON'T think I'll win the Lottery,' said the chap in the pub. 'There were two pens on the Lottery stand at the newsagent and I couldn't even pick the one that worked.'

OUR mention of odd newspaper headlines reminds Norman McLean in Ayr of seeing a picture in a newspaper of the new Moderator of the General Assembly of the Church of Scotland descending the steps of the Assembly Hall while flanked by applauding ministers. The picture was captioned 'New Moderator clapped out'.

BOB Forsyth in Uplawmoor tells us of attending a Burns supper where the chairman was teetotal. Says Bob: 'He was determined to do the right thing when the piper played in the haggis and had arranged with the hotel staff to provide him with two glasses – one with the cratur and the other with cold tea. When the moment arrived he gave a glass to the piper and took one himself and duly toasted the haggis.

'The look on his face when he inadvertently quaffed the goodly measure of whisky was nothing compared to that of the piper on scoffing the cold tea.'

TALES of Glasgow and religion reminded a reader of the classic – that is, old – yarn of the charismatic preacher visiting Glasgow. He asked a young man in the congregation what was bothering him. 'My hearing,' the chap replied.

So the preacher laid his hands over the young fellow's ears, asked the congregation to pray with him to God, took his hands away and asked the man:

'How is your hearing now?'

'I don't know,' the chap replied. 'I'm not due at the sheriff court until tomorrow.'

A READER says when he was at Sunday School he thought the teacher had said that Jesus had been put to his death, not by Pontius Pilate, but an 'unconscious pilot'.

'Until I was twelve,' he tells us, 'I thought Jesus had died in a helicopter accident.'

WE are always impressed by the lengths the clergy will go to at funerals in order to be as positive as they can about the departed. An Ayrshire reader tells us she witnessed her parish priest trying to get round the infrequent visits to church by the deceased, by declaring in his eulogy: 'Mary never completely lost her faith – she never missed an edition of *Songs of Praise*.'

OUR tale of the church service reminds Gerry Burke in Dumbarton of the yarn:

'Wee fella, returning home in back seat of the car in surly, uncommunicative mood, after baby sister's baptism in local church, resists repeated attempts by Dad to source the problem.

'Finally, in high dudgeon, the lad explains, "The priest said he was glad we were going to be brought up in a nice, Christian home. But I want to stay with you."'

A READER told us of a Scottish funeral service where the poignancy of the occasion was enhanced by a lone piper playing a lament outside the church as the mourners went in. The moment was perhaps spoiled, she told us, by a colleague of the deceased, who had flown up from London, who muttered as he saw the piper: 'Damn buskers. Don't they know there's a time and a place?'

A READER wonders about the young girl whom he heard in the supermarket gossiping with her girlfriend. Her pal asked her for more details. The girl then replied: 'I've already told you more than I actually know.'

DUNCAN Cameron, speaking at the St Paddy's Breakfast at the Indigo Hotel in Glasgow, said he was once told by Irish rugby legend Willie John McBride of a train stopped at Limerick station with the guard walking through the carriages shouting: 'Is there an Irish priest on board?'

When he got no response, he was approached by a

Presbyterian minister who came out of the first-class carriage and asked if he could be of assistance, fearing it was a matter of life or death.

'I don't know,' said the guard. 'Do you have a bottle opener?'

READERS never realised how educational the BBC was until the BBC Scotland news website told of accidents on an icy Lanarkshire motorway before adding: 'It is believed that ice formed when temperatures fell below freezing.'

'Who said investigative journalism was dead?' asks reader Ronnie McLean.

A PERTHSHIRE reader swears to us that when leaving church on Sunday he heard a fellow worshipper tell the minister as he shook his hand that his sermon hadn't been very good that day.

The minister looked shocked, so the parishioner's wife told the minister: 'Just ignore him. He doesn't know what he's talking about. All he does is repeat what he hears other people saying.'

22

Gone But Not Forgotten

Fond memories of those who are no longer with us.

STRESSFUL time, funerals. A reader tells us of a recent Glasgow funeral where a young relative of the deceased stopped the priest before the coffin was being taken into the chapel and said he wanted to place a picture of his late aunty's pet dog on the casket. The priest gently squeezed the chap's arm and told him: 'It's a coffin, son – no' a sideboard.'

CHRIS Thornhill in Ardfern tells us about the Highland funeral in winter when the two gravediggers were standing to one side, stamping their feet and patting their arms to try to keep warm, while waiting for the end of the graveside service.

As the mourners turned to leave, one of them approached the cold gravediggers and asked: 'Do you chaps take a dram?'

When they eagerly answered in the affirmative, the

mourner pointed back at the grave and told them: 'Well, let that be a dreadful warning to you.'

GOOD to see Glasgow journalist, humorist and songwriter, the late Cliff Hanley, featuring in the latest edition of the *Oxford Dictionary of National Biography*.

We were once told that it was Cliff, a proud former pupil of Eastbank Academy, who claimed his house was broken into and the police officer laboriously took down the details of what was stolen, pausing when Cliff included 'my dux medal'.

The officer asked with some astonishment: 'What did your duck do to get that?'

SAD to hear of the death in 2013 of Celtic's Sean Fallon, Jock Stein's right-hand man. We recall the story of Stein being seriously injured in a car crash and Fallon taking charge of the team. He visited Stein in hospital where the great man could not speak. Instead Stein scribbled in a notepad asking how the team had performed.

Fallon wrote down a reply about the team doing well and handed back the pad. Stein scribbled furiously away and wrote, with a few expletives, that, while he couldn't speak, he could still hear perfectly well.

THE death of Chic Murray's wife and fellow performer Maidie reminded Matt Vallance of when there was a fire in the Edinburgh hotel that Chic and Maidie owned and managed. Chic told a newspaper reporting on it: 'I can honestly say, in all the years we've been married, it's the first time I've ever seen the wife take a bucket.'

SCOTS comedian Vladimir McTavish recalled how, after the death of fellow comedian Malcolm Hardee, his brother was at his flat sorting his affairs when the phone rang. It was the Inland Revenue asking when Malcolm was going to settle his tax bill. When his brother informed the caller that Malcolm had died the week before, the chap said, 'Really, Mr Hardee, that's what you told us last year.'

IAN Brock in Bearsden tells us about an organist at a funeral playing the rousing 'Dam Busters March' as the mourners were leaving the crematorium.

When the undertaker asked why he chose the music

the organist rather smugly replied that he had noticed the deceased had a floral arrangement spelling out Biggles and assumed that was his nickname as a former RAF pilot.

The undertaker shook his head and told the organist: 'You were half correct. It was a nickname – he was known as Big Les.'

THE death of jazz clarinettist Acker Bilk reminds readers of the old joke of the distressed lady having a bath, who has her big toe stuck in the tap and cannot free it. Her husband calls a plumber, and at the last minute throws her a bowler hat to protect her modesty.

'Can you help?' he anxiously asks the plumber.

'Well, I can free the lady's toe. That's not a problem. But I'm afraid Acker Bilk's a goner.'

AFTER the death of that great golfer Arnold Palmer, a colleague recalled: 'I met him at a dinner at Royal Troon in the 1980s prior to The Open. He revealed that as a previous winner of The Open at Troon he had been made an honorary member of the club. He was then sent a demand for a £650 levy to put the new roof on the clubhouse. Being a much classier dude than those running the club, he sent them a cheque.'

WHEN radio presenter Sir Jimmy Young passed away we were reminded of a *Herald* interview when he was asked about the most stupid thing he had done, and thrice-married Jimmy replied:

'Marrying my second wife. We were having an affair and she told me that didn't mean I had to marry her.

'However, when I was young my father told me, "If a woman is good enough to sleep with, she is good enough to marry." Dad's advice was pretty stupid. I should have taken hers.'

MIXED views on Hugh Hefner, founder of the *Playboy* magazine who died at the age of ninety-one. One reader does make the interesting point, though: 'It shows you how long Hugh Hefner lived that his first wife's name was Mildred, and his last wife's name is Crystal.'

MUCH sadness across the football community with the death of Lisbon Lion captain for Celtic, Billy McNeill. We recall Billy at a *Herald* book event telling the audience that the basic wage when Celtic won the European Cup in 1967 was forty quid a week. The next year, the players sent Captain Billy in to see formidable manager Jock Stein about a rise.

Says Billy: 'I eventually came back to the players and told them, "Well I did my best, but you know what the Big Man's like, no chance."

'The real story is that I went in, said the lads thought they were due a wage rise, and Big Jock said, "F*** off." There was no point in arguing with him. I then went and sat in the toilet for half an hour so that the lads would think we had at least had meaningful negotiations.'

THE death of ebullient former TV racing tipster John McCririck reminds us of when he was hired to make a cameo appearance in the Scottish comedy series *Still Game*.

John arrived for filming at a race day at Lingfield Park, looked around and declared there were not enough punters there to make it look busy and suggested they go for lunch first. After a very long and very enjoyable lunch – courtesy of the BBC of course – John finally agreed there was enough of a crowd, and went out to be filmed.

AND reader Gerry MacKenzie tells us: 'A good few years back, John turned up in Milngavie town centre to do the opening honours for a new branch of one of the big national bookmaker's chains. He regaled the assembled punters with amusing stories, cut the tape and then advised them to stash every penny they had in their possession on a nag he named, due to race in twenty minutes' time. He assured them it was a "dead cert". The punters did so. The nag coasted it. The new manager was sick as the proverbial parrot.'

A READER recalls when Scotland's great panto star Johnny Beattie visited his golf club to play a celebrity pro-am. An obviously nervous Johnny swung on the first tee while a large crowd watched. He then suffered the indignity of missing the ball. He simply shouted: 'Bloody hard course, this.'

SIR David McNee, who has sadly died, was involved in high-profile events as Metropolitan Police Commissioner, but there were humbler cases when he was a beat bobby in Glasgow's Partick – such as the time he booked sixteen youths for playing football at four in the morning. He felt the noise was unfair on folk trying to sleep, but knowing they might simply run away he gathered up their jackets which they had put down for goals. As they queued up for their jackets he booked them, apart from one jacket-less lad who ran away.

Constable McNee followed him home where he was hiding in the staircase cludgie. As David dragged him off, the lad's mother attacked David in the street with such ferocity her nightgown fell off, with the lad shouting: 'Look what you've done to my mam!'

OUR mention of plans to create a memorial to the late miners' leader Mick McGahey reminds Dan Edgar in Rothesay:

'My sadly departed friend, the late, great Jimmy Reid, once told me about enjoying a dram with Mick in a London pub after a busy day of union business. Two whiskies arrived on their table. McGahey complained to the barman, 'There's a fly in my glass'.

'The barman apologised profusely with McGahey replying,

"The fly is no' really the problem – the fact that it can walk aboot is!'"

WE were sad to hear of the death of radio presenter Nicholas Parsons, surely the most unlikely performer ever to have worked in a Glasgow shipyard. His urbane charm wasn't manufactured or false, as Dorothy-Grace Elder discovered when she sat down to record an interview with him for BBC Scotland.

During the interview a colleague appeared, appealing to Dorothy-Grace to help with an emergency on another programme. Dorothy-Grace looked despairingly at Nicholas, who in his unruffled and sympathetic way said: 'Give me your question list. I'll do the answers and you can put your own voice on the tape later.'

Nicholas interviewed himself splendidly, and was even rather tough on himself at one point.

A FOND recollection of novelist, poet and painter Alasdair Gray, who sadly died in 2019. Back in the bitterly cold January of 2002, when black ice was everywhere, the writer Bernard MacLaverty bumped into Alasdair and his wife Morag walking into the pub. Alasdair was carrying a sizeable, rolled hearth-rug beneath his arm. 'It's to help Morag over the more difficult bits,' he told Bernard.

SAD to hear of the death in 2011 of retired football commentator David Francey, whose distinctive passionate voice was always recognisable.

The story was told that BBC Scotland in the 1970s held a David Francey soundalike competition.

David himself secretly sent in a tape – and came third. The winner simply repeated 'Jimmy Johnstone' in frantic Francey-style diction for three minutes without pausing.

AND John Scott in Port Glasgow recalls: 'David Francey was once commentating from a table at the side of the pitch.

'Suddenly there was a thump, followed by silence, then after some seconds he came back with the words, "Sorry for the break in commentary. I have just been hit in the face with the ball. I don't know who it was yet, but he won't be having a very good game the next time I'm commentating."'

SAD to hear of the death in 2014 of comedy actor Rik Mayall, who was still in his fifties. Arguably his best role was as the amoral and devious Conservative politician Alan B'Stard in *The New Statesman*. The show's producer John Bartlett was once asked if it was time for a sequel and he replied: 'There was a sequel to Alan B'Stard. It was called Tony Blair, but it wasn't quite as believable and certainly not as funny.'

THE late great folk singer Danny Kyle once travelled overnight to Glasgow after a gig in the north of England and was desperate for breakfast. Although it was five in the morning Danny spotted a greasy spoon that was open, rushed in and ordered a full breakfast and a cup of coffee.

When the coffee arrived he took a large gulp and smilingly told the waitress it tasted like nectar. 'Well, if you don't like it, you don't have to drink it,' she replied.

THE late Bruce Forsyth was of course a keen golfer, and in the 1970s he took part in a pro/celebrity golf match at Gleneagles which included Sean Connery, Bing Crosby and Burt Lancaster. Bruce later recalled that there was a reception and dinner afterwards in the hotel, and the following morning the hall porter found actor George C. Scott asleep in a chair, still wearing his dinner suit.

When the porter gently woke him and asked if he could get him anything, George C. replied: 'Get me a cab. I'm going home.'

'What about your clubs, Mr Scott?' continued the porter.

'Burn 'em,' said the actor.

FOLK were recalling the humour of the late Ken Dodd, and Tom Peck told us:

'Ken was on the Michael Parkinson show where he explained, "If you tell a joke in Glasgow, they laugh. In Birmingham, they don't."

When Parky asked, "Why's that?" he replied, "They can't hear it."'

23

A Sporting Life

Sport is never far from the thoughts of many a Scot and luckily they can even laugh about it.

ONE of the first people to buy a copy of Celtic footballer Neil Lennon's autobiography, *Man And Bhoy*, was BBC sports reporter Chick Young. A smiling Neil at the book-signing in the Celtic Superstore asked Chick who he should make out the dedication to.

'To the lucky winner on eBay,' replied Chick.

A CHAP in an Ayrshire golf club was telling his pals that when he got a hole-in-one he went home and told his wife: 'I think that's my greatest ever achievement.'

She replied: 'What about your three children?'

He only realised later he had totally missed her point as he told her: 'You're right. I should phone and tell them.'

BEFORE a crucial Celtic–Rangers game, a fan announced in the pub:

'The wife has to go into hospital for a small procedure, and she asked me to go with her. I told her it clashed with the Old Firm game and she said, "Can you not tape it?"

'I told her that was an excellent suggestion, but was she sure the hospital would allow her to take a camera and tripod in?'

WE mentioned the very best of horse racing taking place at the Cheltenham Festival and a reader tells us:

'I had a few pals around for poker and I said to the guy who won the most, "How come you're lucky at cards, but you're so unlucky at picking winners at Cheltenham?"

'"I don't get to shuffle the horses," he replied.'

FORMER Ayr United captain Johnny Graham recalled playing against Rangers, and upbraiding the linesman for giving all the offside decisions in favour of the Glasgow side.

Later, when Johnny took a corner and hoisted the ball straight out of play, the linesman standing beside him at the corner flag merely commented: 'And you say I'm having a bad game?'

A WEST END reader attending a Partick Thistle match heard a young chap ask a scarf seller how much they were, and was told they were £7. 'I'll give you a tenner for two of them,' the fan then offered.

'This is Maryhill,' the vendor replied. 'No' the kasbah.'

SIR Alex Ferguson, giving a lecture on leadership at the Royal College of Physicians and Surgeons of Glasgow, told his audience of a quiz between coaching staff and players on a foreign trip. The coaches were leading, with one question to go, when the players were asked which artist painted sunflowers.

Given the blank looks from the players, the coaches were confident of victory, only for Nicky Butt to shout out 'Van Gogh!'

Sir Alex, who does not take kindly to losing, barked: 'How the hell did you know that?'

Nicky replied: 'I have two in my house.'

NEXT year is the fiftieth anniversary of Partick Thistle beating Celtic 4–1 in the League Cup final. A glorious win, but a little vignette we remember from that day – the Thistle team, followed by a camera crew, returned to their Firhill ground after the game to celebrate.

As the players stood outside Firhill it soon became apparent that no one could find the key to let them in.

As one Jags player said: 'I could have become a professional footballer or joined the circus. With Thistle you can do both.'

GOLF can turn many players into philosophers. One keen golfer told us the truism: 'If your opponent has trouble remembering whether he took a six or a seven, he probably took an eight.'

THE late *Herald* editor Arnold Kemp once told of phoning the then Tory Scottish sports spokesman, MP Hector Munro, for a quote for the paper after boisterous Scottish football fans invaded the pitch at Wembley after an England game and then dug up parts of the pitch. 'Good for them! Tell them to bring me back a lump!' declared Hector.

A few minutes later Hector's wife called Arnold back and said that what Hector had meant to say was: 'This kind of thuggish behaviour disgraces Scotland and must be stopped.'

TOUGH times for Partick Thistle just now. When former Lisbon Lion Bertie Auld was their manager in the 1970s he got them promoted from the old First Division to the Premier League.

At his first press conference of the new season he told the press that they had a great chance of winning a major European competition. As the press attempted to digest that claim he added: 'We've still to write the song, though.'

WE pass on an interview with former Manchester United player Diego Forlan on a pre-season tour of America where there was a tennis court where they were staying, and he challenged star striker Ruud van Nistelrooy to a game. He added that only manager Sir Alex Ferguson knew Diego had been a junior tennis star before turning to football.

When asked what Sir Alex did, he said: 'He was betting money on me.'

TENNIS star Andy Murray was interviewed by some school pupils in Glasgow with one asking if his mum Judy got upset with him occasionally swearing on court. Andy turned to see if Judy was in earshot before replying: 'It was my mum I picked it up from.'

PLANS have been submitted to knock down the Old College Bar on Glasgow's High Street. We recall when a group of Celtic players called in briefly to chat to the old regulars, with a couple of players accepting an invitation to sit down and have a game of dominoes.

We like the way such simple stories grow arms and legs, as a few days later a tabloid reporter arrived and asked the barman: 'So, is it true what they say? Is Chris Sutton really a member of the domino team here?"

BILL Lothian was playing in a seniors golf tournament at Dunbar which was a 'shotgun foursomes' where eighteen groups start off on different tees at the one time, signalled in the past by firing a shotgun that everyone could hear.

Says Bill: 'Organisers said it would be launched by the sound of a horn, then explained in the pre-competition instructions, "We have tried launching a rocket to let everybody know when to start, but unfortunately this led to the Dunbar lifeboat being wrongly called out."'

IT'S been a while since Scotland has been in a World Cup final so we simply pass on the observation of Sarah Simmer: 'If you think asking a Scottish person, "How are Scotland doing in the World Cup?" will shake them in any way, you have fundamentally misunderstood the collective character of Scottish people, who have long ago transcended any hopes of "victory" in any aspect of life. We're past that.'

THE news story about a statue being unveiled to Lisbon Lion Bobby Lennox reminds entertainer Andy Cameron:

'The charity side Dukla Pumpherston were playing down south and on the bus somebody suggested that Bobby entertain the company. A Rangers player bet Bobby that he couldn't sing 'The Sash'.

"'Of course, ah can," says Bobby and started, "*Sure it's old and it is beautiful*" then stopped. He then explained, "That's all ah know because at that point we always scored – and the Rangers supporters shut up."'

OUR favourite golf gag – the golfer who, come hail or shine, got up every Saturday morning at seven to play a round at his club. But one weekend when he reached the door, the biting cold rain was almost horizontal and for once he put his golf bag down, undressed and quietly slipped back into bed with his half-asleep wife and told her: 'The weather's terrible.'

Sleepily she replied: 'Can you believe my husband's out golfing in that?'

A FEMALE player at Airdrie Golf Club recalls phoning to *The Herald*'s sports pages some years ago with the competition results of the ladies section, which included who had won the May Cup.

It appeared in the paper as the Makeup Winner.

A MILNGAVIE golfer told us that the golf club at Balmore, the village between Milngavie and Kirkintilloch, has won the local league for senior players for the first time. The euphoric members were joshing that perhaps they should hire an open-top bus to celebrate. A club member later declared:

'I contacted a local bus company who told me, "We don't have much call for these buses up here in Scotland, sir." He then added, "I think we once had a provisional booking from a Mr A. Salmond back in 2014 . . . but he never came back to us."'

WE remember former referee Brian McGinlay officiating in Spain when his linesman was hit by a pomegranate thrown from the crowd. Writing the match report, Brain wasn't convinced his spelling of pomegranate was correct, and neither of his linesmen were sure.

So, his report to FIFA explained: 'My linesman was struck on the head with an orange.'

SURELY time for another daft old golf joke, says a reader in a Pringle sweater. Well, what about the married couple who were playing on the ninth green when the chap's wife collapsed with a groan, pleading for help? Hubby calls 999 on his mobile, talks to a few folk, then picks up his putter to take his shot.

His prostrate wife gasps: 'I'm dying over here and you're putting?'

'Don't worry, dear,' he replies, 'they found a doctor on the second hole and he's coming to help you.'

'How long will it take him to get here?' she asks feebly.

'Not long,' says her husband. 'Everybody's agreed to let him play through.'

RALPH Topping, the retired chief executive of betting firm William Hill's, said that no matter how tough business gets, it would never be as hair-raising as when he worked as a teenager in a branch in Glasgow's Govan.

A punter, upset at a mix-up over which horse he had backed, threatened to end Ralph's relatively short life, before storming out.

Ralph was telling everyone that those who make the loudest threats never carry them out, when the chap returned with a Japanese ceremonial sword with which he slashed at Ralph through the gap below the protective screen.

As six-foot-plus Ralph leaped back from the lethal swipes, his five-foot-nothing Govan cashier went round the front and she bellowed: 'Right, get oot, ya bampot' – which the chap did.

OUR story of the cleaner who was struggling to understand the Scots word 'stoor' reminds Rob Parker in Edinburgh of when he was playing in a football tournament in America and his team's manager, a Glaswegian, felt that after a stoppage the referee should be restarting the game with a dropped ball rather than conceding a free kick to the opposition.

Rob still recalls the blustering, red-faced manager screaming at the referee: 'It's a stoat up! Stoat it! Stoat the baw!'

'Needless to say,' says Rob, 'the confused referee merely smiled and got on with the game.'

FORMER R&A captain Colin Brown was recalling his own sporting past when he spoke at the Trades House of Glasgow.

Colin in his younger days turned out for Clydesdale Cricket Club, which once went on tour in Ireland, with the day ending in a dance at which he was whirled around the floor by an enthusiastic Irish girl.

Apologising for his lack of dancing skill, Colin told her: 'I'm a little stiff from bowling.'

'Oh, I couldn't care less where you're from,' she happily told him.

WE mentioned the anniversary of England's 1961 victory over Scotland 9–3 at Wembley and we were reminded of Rangers player Bobby Shearer later explaining: 'England cheated. They used an orange ball, which goalie Frank Haffey of Celtic refused to go near, and which neither Eric Caldow nor I would kick.'

DREADFUL result for Scotland at Hampden against the Czech Republic. Murray Robertson had taken his partner's nine-year-old son, whose father is Norwegian, to the game. As they walked away from the park, an auld fella ruffled the youngster's hair and told him not to worry about it.

'It's okay,' replied the young Norwegian. 'I was told that if I'm going to support Scotland I'll have to be prepared for disappointment.'

SPORTS journalist Robert Philip, in his book *Scottish Sporting Legends*, tells the tale of legendary Liverpool manager Bill Shankly berating forward Tony Hateley for his lack of talent. Defending himself, Tony replied: 'You have to admit I'm great in the air.'

But Shankly barked back: 'I'll grant you that, son, but so

was Douglas Bader and he had two better legs than you'll ever have.'

AH, female logic. Former Aberdeen footballer Duncan Shearer told in his autobiography, *Shearer Wonderland*, of six players on a pre-season trip to Austria being fined for staying out boozing until four in the morning.

Duncan was feeling smug when he phoned his wife as he was not one of the six. Instead, the first thing she asked was how come he and pal Billy Dodds were not involved as it was not like them to miss a good night out, so what had they been up to?

TALES of the much-missed Glasgow football team Third Lanark, with Martin Milarky telling us:

'As a ball boy at Cathkin, I witnessed many strange

incidents. After the match, players, club officials and ball boys, amazingly, gathered in the lounge to partake of sausage rolls, but it was also where the Hi-Hi players were paid. Even as an eleven-year-old, I knew it was wrong to see the great Thirds and later Celtic goalie Evan Williams paid his £8 wage by having sixty-four half-crowns from the gate money counted out while he juggled a sandwich and a cup of tea.

'Meanwhile, friends and cronies of chairman Bill Hiddleston knocked back the champagne feet away.'

A READER once heard a fan discussing his trip to an away game in the SPL, and how he managed to cadge a lift back on a supporters' bus.

'So they had a spare seat?' asked his pal.

'Aye,' the chap replied. 'It was full originally, but fortunately someone got lifted.'

AMERICAN sports website Soccerly interviewed Partick Thistle's Mexican player Gabriel Piccolo about playing in Scotland – the answer being that he'd like to wear gloves because it's so cold, but doesn't think it's the right image for a centre-back. Anyway, when asked what it was like walking into the Firhill dressing room – they called it 'locker room' – for the first time, he told them:

'I thought they were speaking French or German. I was like "Are they speaking English, really?" I didn't understand anything in the first two weeks.'

FRENCH club St Etienne is buying the old Hampden football posts for its museum, as the club always argued it was the old-fashioned square posts which denied the team the European Cup when they played in the final at Hampden in 1976. It was a memorable final.

As my colleague Tom Shields put it: 'I recall the social aftermath when a follower of St Etienne, known as Les Verts, sporting a green and white top hat, was drowning his sorrows, being bought pints and chatting up the girls in a heavy Maurice Chevalier accent. He was, of course, a chancer from Maryhill.'

THE nights are fair drawing in, which can only mean that the annual dinners of rugby clubs and golf clubs are not far away. A reader tells us of attending one such boisterous gathering at a rugby club where the guest speaker was droning on interminably. One unruly guest could stand it no longer and threw a bread roll at the speaker, but hit the chairman of the event, who was sitting next to him, squarely on the head. The chairman merely stood up and announced: 'Hit me again – I can still hear him.'

A READER at a Dollar Academy dinner was much taken with guest speaker Iain Milne, the former international rugby player, explaining that he was capped forty-four times for Scotland. His brother Kenny was capped thirty-nine times for his country. Their brother David managed only one cap for Scotland.

'Or as he likes to tell people,' explained Iain, 'he's one of the three Milne brothers who between them have played eighty-four times for Scotland.'